BACK OFF

Cool Down, Try Again

Teaching Students How to Control Aggressive Behavior

by Sylvia Rockwell

PUBLISHED BY THE COUNCIL FOR EXCEPTIONAL CHILDREN

Library of Congress Cataloging-in-Publication Data

Rockwell, Sylvia.
    Back off, cool down, try again : teaching students how to control
aggressive behavior / by Sylvia Rockwell.
      p. cm.
    Includes bibliographical references (p.   ).
    ISBN 0-86586-263-X
    1. Problem children—Behavior modification—United States.
2. Aggressiveness (Psychology)   3. Social skills—Study and
teaching—United States.   I. Title
    LC4801.5.R63   1995
    371.93'0973—dc20

            95-22433
            CIP

ISBN 0-86586-263-X

Copyright 1995 by The Council for Exceptional Children, 1920 Association Drive,
Reston, Virginia 22091-1589.

Stock No. P5120

Printed in the United States of America

10   9   8   7   6   5   4   3   2   1

With love and a tremendous sense of gratitude, this book is dedicated to two of the most positive people in my life, John M. Rockwell and Eleanor C. Guetzloe.

My husband, John, patiently endures intermittent periods of single parenting while I work. In addition, this confirmed "neat freak" has learned to ignore stacks of books, research articles, notes, and pieces of manuscript scattered about the bedroom and living room. Without his willingness to enter into a true partnership, much of the work I do would not get done. His support in word and action is remarkable.

Dr. Eleanor Carden Guetzloe serves as a professional mentor, mother, and friend. Her ability to accept her students as they are, hold a vision of who they can become, and work with them toward that end is a wonderful model for teachers to emulate. Her life is an inspiration. Her love, sense of humor, and depth of knowledge are precious gifts.

Contents

Introduction

Alice laughed, "There's no use trying," she said. "One can't believe impossible things."

"I dare say you haven't had much practice," said the Queen. "When I was your age I always did it for half an hour a day. Why, sometimes I've believed as many as six impossible things before breakfast."—Lewis Carroll

Teachers who work with students exhibiting emotional and behavioral disorders (EBD) believe, like the Queen, in things others think are impossible. They embrace students others have feared, disliked, or simply considered unteachable. It is with a great deal of appreciation for colleagues who regularly believe at least six impossible things before breakfast that I begin this book.

A therapeutic group development model must integrate theories, instructional strategies, and behavior management. Each component of a program is dependent on the strength of the other components and their compatibility with each other, with the students they are intended to serve, and with the teacher. The adventure of living through the inevitable chaos of a group's beginning to the remarkable creativity of its growth is truly an Alice-in-Wonderland-like process. To those with the skills, courage, love, and faith necessary to begin the journey comes a mixed blessing of burdens and enlightenment. These children demand a teacher's very best; they simply will not thrive without it. The trip is often rocky, but never boring. For me, the trip has continued to be more than worth the effort for almost twenty years.

The following anecdote illustrates a typical verbal exchange during a group's first attempts to establish itself. A list of the questions this book will answer regarding the teacher's role in fulfilling the changing needs and demands of the group brings this section to a close while focusing anecdotal and theoretical information on the eight issues targeted. The students described in the anecdotal sections are composites of many. Any sense of familiarity with individuals that might occur is due to the commonality of behavior patterns presented.

"Shut up, Whore!"

"Who you calling a whore? Slut!"

"Jo, Trina, that's a warning. You can express your feelings without name calling. Jo, rephrase please."

"Be quiet! You don't know anything about me or my mother, so just keep your lies to yourself!"

"That's better, Jo. You told Trina exactly what you felt the problem was without using profanity or name calling. Now, Trina, it's your turn."

"Oh, my God! She just called me a whore and you want me to rephrase. You got me bent!"

"It's your choice, Trina. You can rephrase and take a 5-minute cool-off, or you can refuse to rephrase, fill out a Think Sheet, do a 15-minute sit out, and then rephrase before earning any further points or reward activities."

"You're full of shit if you think I'm going to rephrase anything for you or that raggedy little bitch over there. You can both go fuck yourselves!"

Jo rushes toward Trina with her fist clenched, ready to fight. I step between Jo and Trina and ask Ms. Haines, my associate, to escort Jo to another room for her cool-off.

"Jo, you did a great job of rephrasing. Just go in the next room for 5 minutes while I talk with Trina."

Before I can attempt to talk further with Trina, Mark and Carl decide to get into the act. Ms. Haines manages to usher Jo out the door before Trina can get to her. Mark and Carl, however, are disappointed that a fight didn't occur.

Mark shouts, "Just get Ms. Rockwell instead of Jo."

Carl adds, "Yeah, she shouldn't be butting into your business anyway."

"Mark and Carl, this problem is between Trina and me now. Trina is capable of handling her own business without your assistance. Please take a seat and complete your dioramas while Trina and I talk."

"Shut up, butt face!" This is Trina's response to the boys. I silently say a word of thanks that my attempt to support Trina worked. With Ms. Haines out of the room, I really didn't need three students angry with me at once.

Ann, Tory, Carlos, and Anthony are busy with their dioramas for our culture fair exhibit. With Trina's insult and four classmates on task, Mark and Carl can return to work and still save face. I make a mental note to deal with Mark's and Carl's disruption later. Right now, Trina needs immediate attention.

Skills in managing groups of students with behavioral and emotional problems are more complex than skills required for managing individuals. The power, personality, strengths, needs, and development of a group must be understood and effectively managed against a backdrop of each individual within the group. As educators, we are often well schooled in how to assess and plan for individuals, but poorly prepared for what occurs when individuals are placed in groups.

As the story of this middle school class of students with severe emotional and behavioral problems unfolds, the following questions will be answered:

1. What are the typical developmental stages of emotional, social, and cognitive growth for the average child and adolescent?

2. How can information about individuals be combined to support both individual and group needs?

3. What are the stages of group development for classes with students who exhibit severe emotional and behavioral problems?

4. What is the teacher's role at each stage of the group's development?

5. How is group management different from individualized behavior management?

6. What are the group management skills that teachers need?

7. Which affective programs and academic instructional strategies are most effective at each stage of the group's development?

8. What kinds of planning, recordkeeping, and consultation will be necessary for effective group development?

Although the anecdotal sections of this book represent middle school students, grades 1 through 12 are addressed in the developmental tables, behavior management strategies, instructional techniques, and group development stages. The illustration of middle school behavior through the anecdotal vignettes is representative of student behaviors in younger as well as older classes.

As Chapter 1 begins, Trina is faced with a decision. Throughout life, choices are presented and decisions are made. Typical developmental stages of emotional, social, moral, and cognitive growth must be understood in order to provide a base for responding to individual as well as group issues. The teacher's responsibility in every interaction is to facilitate growth through a series of informed choices.

1

Individual and Group Assessment

What I like about experience is that it is such an honest thing. You may take any number of wrong turnings; but keep your eyes open and you will not be allowed to go very far before warning signs appear. You may have deceived yourself, but experience is not trying to deceive you. The universe rings true wherever you fairly test it.—C. S. Lewis

"Trina, I know you're really angry. Jo said some things you didn't like."

"Yeah, the little tramp! Why are you talking to me? She's the one with the sewer mouth. But, you just yell at me while the little baby, Jo, gets to go with Ms. Haines. I'm not afraid of you. And you can just kiss my ass if you think I'm going to suck up to some teacher!"

Trina is really on a verbal rampage. The rest of the class is beginning to snicker.

"Class, thanks for helping each other out by staying on task. We'll be going to lunch in 10 minutes. Those of you who decide to continue working quietly will earn Bingo with prizes the last 15 minutes of fifth period.

Trina, you have a decision to make. I know you're not afraid of me; and you're not here to please me. That's not the point. If you continue to talk inappropriately, you will not be able to eat lunch with the class, your diorama will not be ready for the culture fair, the field trip you're working toward earning will be in jeopardy, and you'll feel even more angry later. If you sit quietly for 15 minutes, fill out a Think Sheet, and rephrase your comments to Jo, you'll get to lunch only 5 minutes late, earn points toward the field trip, and have time fifth period to finish your diorama. Stop and think about what is best for you."

"Oh, shut up and get me a Think Sheet." Trina slumps into a carrel.

"I'll know that you are ready when you ask appropriately."

"O.K. I'm ready for a Think Sheet."

When Trina has had time to sit quietly and fill out the Think Sheet, we will talk. She and Jo will need time to process the real issues between them as well. For now, I focus on students who are working appropriately as Ms. Haines and Jo slip into the room.

INDIVIDUAL DEVELOPMENTAL STAGES

To understand individual students and respond accurately to their needs, teachers must understand the cognitive, social, emotional, and moral stages of growth for the average student of a particular age. Not everything a student in a classroom for EBD does is a manifestation of a disabling condition. Knowing what is expected for a given age frees the teacher to prioritize issues, thereby saving energy and time.

Table 1.1, showing typical developmental stages for primary, intermediate, middle, and high school aged students, illustrates expected abilities, behaviors, strengths, and weaknesses for each age group.

Students usually develop socially, emotionally, cognitively, morally, and physically within a broad range of age-appropriate norms. Cognitive ability appears to correlate positively with social, emotional, and moral development within the regular education population. Individual profiles on students with behavioral disorders often contain deficit areas. Cognitive development may appear to be at a normal level on intelligence tests, but show significant deficiencies on norm-referenced tests of academic achievement. These students may desire age-appropriate peer relationships, but function emotionally at a level more representative of much younger children, frustrating the development of satisfactory social relationships.

TABLE 1.1
Interpersonal Orientation

Assimilative	*Accommodative*
Level 0 (ages 2–3)	
Screaming	Fear
Tantrums	Running away
Level I (ages 4–6)	
Bullying, bossing, threats, verbal abuse	Acting victimized
Denial, distortion, lying	Lack of assertiveness
One-way fairness	Power-oriented obedience
Level II (ages 7–11)	
Pitting peers against one another	Being a follower
Trickery	Confrontation
Seeking alliances	Asking for help
Friendly persuasion	Reasoning

Level III (ages 12–18)

Group orientation
Expectation of consistency in self and others
Anticipation of others' reactions
Use of humor and perspective as coping mechanisms

Adapted from Selmen, R. L. (1981). The development of interpersonal competence: The role of understanding in conduct. *Developmental Review, 1* 419.

Trina, for example, has an IQ of 115 on an individually administered intelligence test. She functions academically at a fifth grade level in reading, exhibits many of the expected middle school aged desires for peer acceptance and ambivalence toward adult relationships, but has the self-control in social situations of an average 4 year old. Chronologically, Trina is 13 and in the seventh grade. Trina has not started to menstruate and often worries about her small size, lack of hips and breasts, and childlike appearance. Each of these factors combines with many others to shape Trina's individual strengths and weaknesses as well as the educational planning required within the context of the school and classroom group to which Trina is assigned. Some of the additional factors that shape Trina's individual development include family composition, socioeconomic level, family mobility, prenatal and early childhood development, and community involvement. Considering that each of these factors must be evaluated for each of the eight students in the class along with the interactional dynamics of the group, the teacher's job is complex.

Trina was able to regain some self-control once Jo was removed from the room. I supported her ability to make her own decisions when Mark and Carl attempted to encourage her acting-out behavior. As long as the teacher remains firm and supportive, students are usually able to maintain appropriate behavior individually. Dealing effectively with behaviors within the group context requires instantaneous juggling of individual profiles, age-expected norms, and the particular functioning level of the group.

USING THE CLASS PROFILE SHEET

Table 1.1 provides a quick overview of age-equivalent norms for various aspects of development. To establish classroom behavior management plans and coordinate these plans with academic instruction, it is essential to develop a Class Profile Sheet. Before returning to Trina, Jo, and the other students, a look at the Class Profile Sheet (Table 1.2) will provide a wealth of information. A blank copy of the Class Profile Sheet is provided in the Appendix for teacher use.

According to Table 1.1 and information taken from Schurr (1989), middle school aged students typically experience a great deal of conflict over their need for adult approval and their desire to be accepted by peers. Mark's and Carl's comments to Trina and her potential reactions might have been motivated by a simple bid for attention had these students been younger. With younger students, redirecting their attention, offering bonus points for ignoring inappropriate behavior, or even recognition of their desire for attention followed by a promise to be with them shortly might have been sufficient. With middle school students, however, the teacher must remember to assist them in saving face in front of their peers. Appealing to their power to choose rather than a teacher-controlled reward or consequence is one way to show respect for the new and often stressful social-emotional level young adolescents must maneuver.

Before the class arrived on the first day of school, the Class Profile Sheet yielded a wealth of information necessary for academic and behavioral planning. The information on this sheet is gathered from reviewing school records. IQ scores and academic achievement levels are often misleading, but they serve as a starting point in planning. Teachers need to take all information as tentative. There is no real substitute for direct observation. Initial planning can begin, however, by

TABLE 1.2
Class Profile Sheet

Student's Name	Age	Date of Birth	Grade	Morph-ology	IQ	Reading Level	Math Level	Placement Behaviors
Jo	15	10/11	8	Heavy	118	8.5	4.0	Verbal and physical aggression toward staff & peers, truancy, drug use
Trina	13	9/8	7	Small	115	5.0	5.0	Disruptive, verbal aggression, toward staff & peers, refusal to work—noncompliant
Mark	14	7/6	7	Tall	100	5.3	7.0	Verbally aggressive with staff & peers/drug use/theft/disruption
Carl	12	5/5	6	Small	93	3.5	5.0	Instigates fights, off-task, ADHD, runs away from school
Ann	14	10/18	8	Average	87	3.0	3.0	Passive, refuses to work/Low participation/Rarely talks or shows emotion
Tory	12	1/25	6	Average	104	3.0	5.5	Previously placed in class for learning dis-abilities/Aggressive
Carlos	13	3/20	7	Average	98	6.5	6.8	Auditory hallucinations triggered by stress—violent
Anthony	15	6/2	8	Tall	125	10.5	8.9	Truancy. Disrespect toward authority. Threatens—Aggressive when cornered

obtaining preliminary information on students' (a) academic functioning levels, (b) age, (c) referral behaviors, (d) socioeconomic status, (e) morphology, and (f) likes and dislikes. The following analysis of the Class Profile Sheet shown in Table 1.2 was developed as a guide for understanding both individual and group needs for Trina and her classmates.

1. The majority of the class functions in the normal range of intelligence. Two students are above average in this area. Academic lessons will need to be presented orally at a middle school level.

2. Reading levels range from 3.0 to 10.5. Independent work will need to be individualized. Tory is the only student identified as having a learning disability. The differences between Carl's reading and math scores may indicate a disability.

3. Math scores range from 3.0 to 8.9. This will make whole group instruction difficult, but not impossible. Individualized materials and lessons will need to be incorporated into whole group instructional themes.

4. Verbal aggression has a great potential for escalating into physical aggression with this group. Behavior management plans will focus on talk outs, name calling, profanity, put downs, and other forms of verbal harassment. Keeping verbal aggression to a minimum will assist in reducing occurrences of physical aggression, running away, Carlos's auditory hallucinations, and Carl's opportunities to instigate.

5. Jo and Anthony are potential cohorts in truancy plans. Keeping them feeling positively toward school and supportive of each other's appropriate decisions to attend school will be a challenge.

6. Carl and Trina may be at risk due to their small, underdeveloped statures. Alliances with each other to irritate the group or alliances with larger students for protection are both possibilities. Patterns will need to be monitored as the group develops.

7. Mark and Anthony may vie for peer leadership roles. Anthony is a potential peer leader due to his size, age, aggressive tendencies, and intellectual abilities. Mark attends school regularly, however, and may gain the leadership role simply because he is the next in line in terms of size, age, aggression, and status. His peers may tend to hold him in high esteem because of his arrest record. At first glance, Anthony appears to be the better peer leader candidate. His attendance will need to be more regular. The process of selecting and developing a peer leader is discussed in Chapter 3.

8. Carl will need some individual behavior management planning due to his attention deficit with hyperactivity disorder (ADHD). A list of suggested interventions is provided in the Appendix.

9. Carlos will need monitoring due to the psychotropic drugs he is currently taking to help control the auditory hallucinations he experiences.

10. Ann's extreme passivity will be easy to ignore, given the high activity and tension levels of the other students. Careful planning will be necessary to ensure Ann's inclusion in the group.

11. Truancy and running away in response to school stress will need to be addressed openly. Giving priority to referrals to guidance counselors and social workers, parent conferences, academic planning, and behavior management procedures early in the year will protect Jo, Carl, and Anthony from previously established patterns. Other group members will need to be protected from developing new undesirable behaviors.

12. Given the intelligence scores and the findings of several theorists including Piaget (1954) that there tends to be a relationship between affective development and intelligence, many of the strengths, weaknesses, and needs outlined in Table 1.1 for middle school aged students can be expected to occur in this group. Students in classes for EBD, however, also tend to regress to much lower levels of functioning with little or no provocation. Behavior management planning should center around supporting appropriate developmental levels while remaining prepared for regressive tendencies.

Looking at Trina, Jo, and the class as a whole in this way, using the Class Profile Sheet as a guide, will establishing a basis for explanation of the group developmental stages discussed in Chapter 2.

2

Group Developmental Stages

By wise people, an appropriate observation is
accepted even from a child. On the invisibility of
the sun, is not the light of a lamp availed of?
[Sanskrit]—N. Gleason

As Ms. Haines and Jo return to the room, Trina begins to fill out her Think Sheet.

"Jo, are you ready to be with the class?" I ask before allowing her to return to her desk.

"I'm here aren't I?" Jo responds sarcastically.

"What's the matter?"

"Nothing! Just shut up and let me get back to work!"

"Jo, your words and tone of voice tell me that something is wrong. If you're not ready to be a part of the class again, that's OK."

"Fine, I'll just leave again if that's what you want."

"No. That's not what I want. I want you to be successful in here. If there's still a problem, let's deal with it."

"Why'd I have to go out with Ms. Haines? I wasn't the one threatening to fight. Trina was."

"You're right. You made good choices."

"So, why'd I have to leave?"

"Because you were showing the most self-control."

"Oh, great! So, that's how it works. Fine! I'll just punch her out the next time she starts her crap!"

"Jo, I didn't send you out with Ms. Haines to punish you. I sent you out because you were being threatened, and I didn't want anyone to get hurt. The person with the most self-control is the one who can walk away and not get sucked into someone else's problem. I was counting on you to make good choices and be strong. You did it."

"Do I have time in in-class suspension now?"

"No. Trina does for threatening and refusing to rephrase. You said some things in anger that were not appropriate. For that you earned a 0 in appropriate interactions. You chose to rephrase, avoid a fight, and go with Ms. Haines. For that, you earned all your other points for this time period and a thank you! You've already taken responsibility for your choices. You don't need a Think Sheet or in-class suspension time."

"OK. I want to finish my diorama."

"Great! You've got about 5 minutes more before lunch."

As Jo returns to her seat, I ask Carl and Mark to step outside the door. Because I need to be able to monitor the class and speak with students in a semiprivate manner, the one foot in the room, one foot in the hall stance is often useful.

"Look, guys, your interference earlier was not appropriate or helpful to your classmates."

"What are you talking about?" Carl asks in an attempt to appear innocent.

"When Trina and Jo were having a problem, you encouraged Trina to fight and then suggested that she hit me instead."

"Yeah, so. . .? She didn't do it." This time Mark responded defiantly.

"No. Trina used her own good judgment and kept the problem small."

"Yeah, well, even if she had swung on you, you couldn't pin it on us. We're not responsible for her."

"Exactly! You're responsible for you. And your choice was neither appropriate for school nor helpful to your classmates. Encouraging others to hurt people is the same as threatening to do it yourselves. You both earned 0's in appropriate interactions, staying on task, following directions, and ignoring inappropriate peer behavior. Any future attempts to encourage fighting will result in a minimum of 15 minutes in in-class suspension and the completion of a Think Sheet."

"Shit, NO!" Carl screams.

"Hey, man. Calm down." Mark pats Carl once on the back.

"Don't touch me, man." Carl jerks away from Mark. "You gonna take this shit from her?"

"Carl, you have a choice right now. You can accept the four 0's and go to lunch with the class, or you can stay in the room with Ms. Haines. We'll have lunch sent to you. You will not earn points if you remain in the room." I intervened quickly with Carl to take pressure off Mark.

"Come on, Carl. Let's go to lunch. This isn't worth it."

"Thank you for encouraging Carl to make a good decision, Mark. Are you OK with this?"

"Yeah, whatever."

"Yeah, whatever doesn't tell me much, Mark."

"Yeah, I'm fine. Can I just go back to my desk? I'd like to put stuff away before we leave."

"Yes. Thanks for making a good decision." Mark returns to his seat. Now it's Carl's turn.

"OK, Carl, what's your decision?" With Mark gone, no audience, and the prospect of eating lunch in an empty classroom with no one to talk with except an adult, Carl resigns himself to the lesser of two evils—accepting the limits established.

"OK, OK. Can I get my lunch money?"

I flash a thumbs-up signal and a smile. "Yes. Good choice, Carl."

This is only the second week of school. This group is new. They're just beginning to understand and accept the expectations and limits of the situation.

MASLOW'S HIERARCHY

Regardless of the ages and functioning levels of individuals within a group, groups initially function socially at the 2- to 3-year-old level as defined by Selman's (1981) levels of social functioning. Unprovoked acts of aggression, tantruming, screaming, impulsive intrusion, fear, and running away can be expected. Regression to such an immature level of functioning in otherwise intellectually capable individuals would be hard to understand without Maslow's (1962) Hierarchy of Human Needs, which is outlined in Table 2.1. The human organism cannot be motivated to go beyond one level of functioning until previous levels have been satisfied. Physiological needs occupy the lowest level of Maslow's hierarchy. The next level of need is for safety and security. As the table indicates, the need for safety and security is satisfied when there is adequate protection against danger, threats, anxiety, and chaos. To satisfy Maslow's first two levels of human need, the teacher must ensure that students are provided with food and drink, adequate clothing, rest, activity, appropriate lighting, and other physiological comfort considerations while also establishing order, limits, and stability within a firm and nurturing structure.

Students in classes for EBD have by definition failed in other settings. Trust in teachers, peers, and even in themselves is tentative at best. It is not surprising that Stage One group development is so fraught with turmoil. If home, community, and previous school placements have not satisfied physiological, safety, and security needs, then regression in social-emotional functioning is understandable if not inevitable.

The following lunch table discussion illustrates the uncertainty and suspicion with which students greet a new teacher and class.

TABLE 2.1
Maslow's Hierarchy of Human Needs

Needs	Physiological and Psychological Indicators
Level 1: Physiological	Hunger, taste, smell, thirst, sleep, touch
Level 2: Safety and Security	Protection against danger Freedom from fear, chaos, and anxiety Need for structure, order, law, limits, and stability
Level 3: Belonging, Love, and Social Activity	Satisfactory associations with others Belonging to groups Giving and receiving friendship and affection
Level 4: Esteem	Self-respect, achievement, competence, and confidence Deserved respect from others—status, dignity, recognition, and appreciation
Level 5: Self-Actualization or Self-Fulfillment	Achievement of potential Maximum self-development, creativity, and self-expression

Source: Maslow (1962), as cited on a classroom handout from Guetzloe (1993).

"Why'd they put you here?" Anthony asks Carlos as the students settle into their places at the lunch table.

"I don't know. I guess 'cause I punched a teacher." Carlos flips his roll across his plate and smirks at the others.

As the class laughs and offers words of praise for his past indiscretions, I remind them that lunch is a time to discuss positive things. With this reminder from me, Tory snarls back, "What's your problem?"

"No problem here, Tory. I'd just like to keep it that way."

"No, seriously, why are you here? We have to be. But you must be stupid or something!"

Carlos, Mark, Tory, and Carl echo their own forms of agreement on this issue. From their point of view, teachers who willingly accept groups known to have behavior problems are more than a little suspicious. Rational thinking clearly indicates that teachers in EBD classrooms will endure cursing, threatening, chair throwing, destruction of property, multiple attempts to avoid responsibility, and unavoidable conflict. Stupidity and emotional disturbance on the part of the teacher are the only explanations even remotely possible to students who know better than anyone else how bad things can, will, and do get in their worlds.

I see their question as more than fair. Failure on my part to adequately answer that one basic question through thought, word, and action would spell certain disaster for the group. Although my immediate response is only partially accepted pending further proof through appropriate action, my words are heard and remembered.

"I'm here simply because I want to be."

"Yeah, right!" Tory laughs.

"Yeah, right!" I shoot back.

"Yeah, you really love all this crap around here! Get real!" Jo challenges.

"No. I don't love everything. I don't love cursing, fighting, complaining, destruction of property, or lying. I do love watching you grow and being a part of your learning."

"Sure. You're just here 'til a better job opens up." Carlos offers me a way out.

"Carlos, this is the best job already. Where else could I go?"

"Man, what a loser! Teachers don't make no money. How can this be the best job?" Mark questions.

"Money is only part of why people select a job. Money can't buy some things. Just wait. You'll see. This is a great group! You're going to learn more and go farther than you ever imagined!"

"Now I *know* she's crazy!" Tory pats me gently on the back and shakes her head. The others laugh and go on to discuss the movie they watched on television last night. That will not be the last time my motives are challenged. The fact that someone in the group asked about my motives is a good sign. This group has terrific potential for growth. Establishing a dialog with students that is honest, trustworthy, and real is essential.

The preceding anecdotes illustrate many Stage One behaviors. Table 2.2 provides an overview of all three stages of group development.

As Table 2.2 indicates, group development tends to follow predictable patterns of behavior and growth regardless of the functioning levels of individuals within the group. The teacher can facilitate group and individual growth by understanding the essential needs of the group at each stage and responding with supportive, growth-inducing strategies in the behavioral, instructional, affective, and recreational areas.

STEPS FOR FOSTERING GROWTH

Although Erikson (1950), Maslow (1962), Swap (1974), Hewett and Taylor (1980), and others have established hierarchies to illustrate individual development, a comparison between the needs of individuals and those of a group yields useful information. Applied to the broader issues of group development, many of the

TABLE 2.2

Developing Group Dynamics in Classes for Students with Serious Emotional Disturbances

	Affective Instruction	Teacher's Role	Group Development Techniques	Interaction Patterns	Academic and Reinforcement Activities
STAGE ONE (4–12 weeks)	TODDLER NEEDS & BEHAVIORS: • Self-Esteem • Relaxation Techniques	BENEVOLENT DICTATOR 1. Establish control 2. Select a peer leader	Behavior Modification 1. Individual and group profiles 2. Developmental levels	Minimize student-to-student and maximize student-to-adult and adult-to-student interaction	Parallel play that moves students from "I" to "We"
STAGE TWO (4–18 weeks)	PRESCHOOL NEEDS & BEHAVIORS: • Communication • Problem Solving	DIRECTOR 1. Shift control to group 2. Maintain positive authority	Problem-Solving Steps 1. Voting with 3–5 choices 2. Move from authoritarian to democratic	Teacher has central role as clarifier, director, and mediator during whole group	Role play with teacher and student Simple cooking activities or plays Associative play
STAGE THREE (ongoing)	SCHOOL-AGED LATENCY NEEDS & BEHAVIORS: • Social Skills, Refined and Mastered	ARBITRATOR/ FACILITATOR Less and less external control is necessary	Maintain, clarify, and strengthen learned techniques	Wants and needs can be communicated directly between students	Any school and age-appropriate activity (begin mainstreaming)

issues for individuals become modified and magnified. The following are the six basic steps in fostering optimum growth with groups of students who exhibit behavior problems:

1. Take proactive measures in all areas of academic, affective, behavioral, and environmental planning. Begin with strategies that originated from behavior modification and learning theories.

2. Establish positive authority and leadership by meeting and responding to developmental needs while providing necessary supportive structures.

3. Begin to shift from external to internal control with academic and behavior management techniques.

4. Teach social and academic skills necessary for cooperative achievement intellectually, socially, and emotionally.

5. Stabilize and maintain prerequisite cooperative achievement skills.

6. Begin mainstreaming and transitioning.

To develop the information contained in Table 2.2 more completely, the following subsections will describe the needs and behaviors exhibited in Stage One, Stage Two, and Stage Three of group development.

STAGE ONE

Stage One is characterized by frequent and often intense verbal and physical aggression. Most groups exhibit a brief period of calm and compliant behavior initially. This period of calm can last anywhere from a few hours to a few weeks. Every group of students with behavior problems eventually begins to show the teacher and others how its members earned their labels. Teachers would be wise to take the following motto to heart: "Expect the best; but prepare for the worst." Unpredictable acts of aggression occur. The teacher must be ready at all times with two or three back-up plans. Stage One groups need to have expectations and rules stated in clear, concise, concrete terms. They need well-defined and consistently enforced limits. They need to feel respected, protected, and accepted while simultaneously being held accountable for inappropriate behavior.

External methods of controlling behavior are essential. Behavior modification techniques such as the use of rewards and consequences contingent on behaviors are the most efficient ways to establish beginning levels of trust. The use of a supportive behavior modification structure depends heavily on the teacher's ability to stay calm, firm, positive, and realistic with expectations that are predictable, consistent, and fair. Bryngelson (1992) and Morgan and Reinhart (1991) have cited empathy, unconditional positive regard, genuineness, concreteness, and trust as essential traits of teachers who work with groups exhibiting EBD. As Table 2.2 indicates, Stage One groups are actively working to resolve issues of trust. Tuckman (1965) identified group development as occurring in five stages, including (1) forming, (2) storming, (3) norming, (4) performing, and (5) mourning. Forming and storming are effective words to describe individuals' reactions to group involvement as well as the group's overall behavior.

Stage One is the most volatile period in group development. Students usually do not manage student-to-student interactions well without adult monitoring. This stage can be physically and emotionally challenging for the teacher, but it is desirable and worthwhile if managed well. Students who establish a nurturing relationship with an adult who has seen them through their worst acting out and still cares have a foundation of trust to model. Groups cannot reach Maslow's level of belonging unless they feel safe. A teacher who establishes positive control and authority allows the group to feel psychologically and physically safe, which facilitates the development of belonging and group unity.

Because of the challenges involved in managing Stage One behaviors, academic and affective instruction can often appear to be less important. A sense of purpose and mastery, however, needs to be established as part of the overall atmosphere of psychological safety and security. The use of instructional techniques developed in conjunction with behavioral and learning theories provides students with immediate experiences of success. Foundations of knowledge required for higher-level problem solving build students' views of themselves as capable learners. Affective lessons that teach students to recognize and manage their own anger and tension encourage students' feelings of self-control. When behavior management, academic instruction, and affective lessons complement each other and work in response to students' needs, a shift appears in group interactions from "It's me against the world" to "It's us against the world." Stage One can last anywhere from 4 to 12 weeks.

STAGE TWO

Stage Two occurs when the need for external behavior monitoring decreases due to fewer acts of verbal and physical aggression and the acceptance by the group of individual needs and problems without others joining the disturbance. Group problem solving becomes productive at this point as long as the teacher leads the problem-solving process. Students can do what Glasser (1985, p. 125) called "artificial-cooperative learning" tasks such as calling out spelling words to a partner. Structure is still a very necessary component in the success of the group. Students can, however, benefit from opportunities to practice more complex ranges of decision making, problem solving, and communication skills.

It is essential to the development of the group that the teacher respond positively to the students' greater sense of self-control. The Stage One preoccupation with "me" shifts to Stage Two recognition of "us" in terms of group identity, ownership, and pride. Students often begin making statements such as, "We're the best class on the wing" or "We're the academic achievers in this school." A positive group identity can develop only if the teacher has provided ample opportunities for success within a developmentally supportive structure. Hewett and Taylor (1980) emphasized the fact that order, limits, routines, expectations, and rules do not have to be perceived as restrictive and punishing. If these components are combined with a responsiveness to individual and group needs and growth, students establish a positive view of the teacher as an authority and of themselves as members of a well-functioning group.

Stage Two functioning is less volatile than Stage One. The teacher can begin to feel frustrated and confused, however, due to less frequent but often quite intense periods of acting out. During Stage Two, the group needs to test limits to make sure that they are still in place. This is once again a positive period of growth. Maintaining clear limits without overreacting or becoming overly punitive, while simultaneously supporting movement toward internal control, is a balancing feat well worth the effort.

Stage Two can last anywhere from 4 to 18 weeks. A shift from "It's us against the world" to "Let's get into the mainstream" signals an end to Stage Two.

STAGE THREE

Stage Three group functioning is characterized by age-appropriate behaviors. The teacher can get on with teaching as if severe behavior problems never existed. This easygoing atmosphere may not carry over into other settings with different adults. Behaviors are under control enough, however, for the teacher to begin planning for transition experiences.

Stage Three is a wonderful time for students and teachers when it occurs. Not all groups reach Stage Three functioning. Individuals within a group may begin transitioning to less restrictive placements in regular education classrooms before the whole group reaches the maturity of Stage Three processing. Transitioning group members usually have mixed feelings about leaving, as do members who are not quite ready to go. The group is able, however, with teacher assistance, to talk about these mixed feelings and deal with them effectively and creatively.

Regression is expected during transitioning or at earlier stages when stressors occur such as holidays, substitutes, or the addition of new students to the class. The anxiety created by such changes in routines and relationships triggers issues of trust. Some students will withdraw. Others will become unusually sensitive and jealous in their relationships with staff and peers. A few might even revert to verbal and physical aggression. Preparing a class for changes in advance, reducing the number of student-to-student interactions for a brief period, and modifying academic instruction in ways that reinforce feelings of mastery are effective and nonintrusive intervention strategies. Regression rarely lasts long if the teacher provides support through increased structure.

Chapter 3 develops the changing roles teachers must play as groups shift from one stage to the next. Carl opens Chapter 3 with a common Stage One dilemma. That anecdote will be projected into the future to illustrate Stage Two and Stage Three group and teacher responses.

3

The Teacher's Shifting Role

"What is real?" asked the Rabbit one day . . . .

"It's a thing that happens to you. When a child loves you for a long, long time; not just to play with, but Really loves you; then you become real."

"Does it hurt?" asked the Rabbit.

"Sometimes," said the Skin Horse for he was always truthful . . . . "It doesn't often happen to people who break easily, or have sharp edges, or have to be carefully kept . . . ."—M. Williams

"Oh, my God!" Trina screams unexpectedly, shoves her plate across the table and into Anthony's lap, stands, and swats Carl on the back of the head all in one fluid motion. Before I can intervene or even determine the cause of this unexplained explosion, Carl knocks Trina to the floor and Anthony throws Trina's plate across the cafeteria. Fortunately, the class that usually sits near us has already left. Flying food and milk hit the wall, table, and floor, but no people.

Anthony is cursing profusely over the stains on his new shirt. Jo and Tory are angrily coming to Trina's defense as fellow females band together against Carl and Anthony. Ann backs into a corner. Mark and Carlos begin to bang the table with their fists, chanting "Food fight! Food fight!"

Ms. Haines and an associate from another class come to my assistance as I try to decide where to start. The problem began between Trina and Carl. But, without time to find out the details, it quickly became a group problem. I know Ann is upset, but she is in control and within eyesight. I call, "Ann, you're doing a good job. Thanks for moving away from the table." I asked Ms. Haines to take Ann, Mark, and Carlos back to the classroom. At first Mark and Carlos want to stay to watch what they hope will be some action. Ms. Haines again presents them with a choice—loss of privileges for staying or a bonus for moving. They reluctantly return to class. I ask the other associate to take Trina, Jo, and Tory to the girl's restroom to clean up and then to an unoccupied office area to calm down. Even though Carl and Anthony are both extremely angry and capable of aggression, they aren't mad at each other. Trying to get them to leave with an associate might invite further violence. So I think it best to try to verbally de-escalate the situation in the cafeteria with them. I grab napkins, wet them in the water fountain, and hand them to Anthony.

"Here, Anthony. I'm sorry about your shirt. We'll see if the home economics teacher can wash it. I have a t-shirt in the room that you can use until yours is clean."

"That little bitch! She's crazy! What's going on? Shit, man! Look at my shirt!"

"I know. I'm sorry. Try to get as much out as you can at the water fountain while I talk with Carl."

Anthony is starting to get control of himself. He quits screaming. All I can hear is mumbling from him as he tries to clean his shirt. Carl is bouncing around like a prize fighter. He's jumping from the bench to the table top punching the air and screaming obscenities at the top of his lungs.

"Carl, stop." I command.

"Stop! Stop? Shit, Bitch! She hit me and you just stood there. I ought to knock your ass on the floor, too!"

"Carl, you need to sit down. Trina's gone. I want to know what happened."

"What happened? What happened? Are you blind, deaf, and stupid? You saw what happened!"

"I saw her stand, heard her scream, saw her hit you in the head and push her tray into Anthony's lap, but I still don't know what happened. Sit down, Carl. I want to hear from you how the whole thing started." I don't mention that he knocked Trina down, because I don't want to deal with his consequences until he is calm. Reminding him now of his behavior would only start another verbal escalation of anger and denial. Slowly Carl slides to the bench beside me. "OK. Tell me what happened."

"Nothing."

"Nothing? Trina just went crazy suddenly and started screaming, throwing food, and hitting for no reason? Come on, Carl. Trina can get pretty angry, but she usually has a reason."

"Well, I was just joking with her. God! Can't anyone take a joke around here?"

"What was the joke?"

"I just did this." Carl then demonstrates how he pretended to bring up a large wad of phlegm and spit it on her tray. He promises that he really didn't do it; that it was all just an act. Apparently, however, Trina didn't see the humor in this bit of middle school behavior. We have some major problem solving to do.

I explain to Anthony that he needs to clean up the food and milk he threw. He accepts this direction, the points not earned, and a restriction from the cafeteria for 2 days in exchange for a clean shirt and laundry services from the home economics teacher.

Carl and Trina earn 1 day of in-school suspension and 5 days of cafeteria restriction for physical aggression. Carlos, Mark, Jo, and Tory earn a Think Sheet and in-school suspension time for encouraging a problem. And Ann earns time with a staff member of her choice while the others take care of their consequences.

The following discussion of the teacher's role during Stage One describes the delicate balancing of issues the teacher faces at this critical time in the development of relationships with individuals and the dynamics of the group.

STAGE ONE: BENEVOLENT DICTATOR

Teachers have a seemingly contradictory role during Stage One. The term *benevolent dictator* seems to apply. During Stage One, order, limit setting, and structure are essential. Teachers must use external methods of control such as rewards, consequences, token economies, and other behavioral interventions skillfully, positively, predictably, and with immediacy. Stage One is not a good time for cooperative ventures. Most of what happens in the classroom must be carefully controlled by a caring, trustworthy adult. As mentioned in Chapter 1, Bryngelson (1992) has identified five essential conditions in the establishment of a significant relationship with students. Those five include empathy, unconditional positive regard, genuineness, concreteness, and trust. As Maslow's hierarchy (1962) indicates, trust cannot be established without physical and psychological safety. The most efficient way to establish safety is through a well-developed behavior modification program. Hence, Stage One requires a teacher to assert a benevolent dictatorship, taking every possible proactive measure through the following steps:

1. Arrange furniture to meet social-emotional needs as well as instructional and organizational needs.

2. Adjust schedules to provide a balance between highly structured periods and more stimulating activities.

3. Establish a group behavior management plan that incorporates individual needs.

4. Provide direct instruction, programmed learning, and precision teaching lessons. These will build students' self-confidence while establishing a knowledge base from which to expand problem-solving and higher-level thinking skills as students demonstrate readiness for learning experiences that require less external structure.

5. Keep student-to-student interactions to a minimum initially. This is especially important during times when adult monitoring would be difficult. Trust and safety cannot be established if individuals within the group continually undermine each other or the adults with problems created in secret.

6. Provide group-building opportunities that move students from an "I" to a "We" orientation without overstimulating or threatening them. These activities and opportunities are most effective when integrated into the affective, academic, and recreational arenas. Examples will be developed more fully in Chapter 6 and in the Appendix. A few examples include making a class photo album to document important events in the life of the group such as field trips, birthdays, and academic projects; publishing a group anthology of student poetry, art, and stories related to a topic of study; and construction projects that require each person to do a part of the model independently and the group to assemble the parts to make a total display. Cooking activities are also adaptable, reinforcing, and motivating ways to encourage appropriate group participation if planned and executed with student needs as a basis for recipe selection.

7. Select a group peer leader. The group will select a leader whether the teacher assists with this process or not. Bandura (1969, as cited by Alberto & Troutman,

1982) qualities of leadership. These include being perceived as similar to other group members and being reinforced for modeled behavior. Gelfand (1962, as cited by Alberto & Troutman, 1982) found that a demonstrated competence is another important factor in leadership status. The group will select a student they perceive to be strong and similar to them in ways they consider important. The students' perception of important and successful qualities can be drastically different from the teacher's. This student is usually quite capable of using his or her status to control the group during Stage One.

The teacher needs to be aware of the emerging peer leader and assist the group in selecting a leader if two students vie for the position in ways that create overwhelming conflict. The student with the most potential for having a positive influence on the group is the one who has an appropriate goal even if his or her surface behaviors are disruptive. If Anthony came to school more often, he would be a better peer leader than Mark. He is big, strong, and intelligent—verbally aggressive, but rarely physically aggressive. He has not had problems with the law and is committed to his community football league. Mark will have high status with the group, however, because he has a record with the local law enforcement agency, fights frequently and well, and is large for his age. The teacher can help the group select a positive peer leader by rewarding the positive content of this student's responses even if the words are a little rough. For example, Anthony's directive to the group to "Shut the hell up!" so he could finish his work could be rewarded with a response from the teacher such as, "Thanks for your reminder, Anthony" followed by a request that he rephrase his request in a more school appropriate way. The fact that Anthony did not resort to threats of physical violence or actual physical aggression can be used as a point of discussion for group affective lessons.

Driekurs, Grumwald, and Pepper (1982) cited four motivations for misbehavior: (1) a need to establish power and control, (2) a need for attention, (3) a need to seek revenge, and (4) helplessness. Responding to the needs underlying a behavior and following up with corrective instruction to assist a student in establishing more successful strategies for meeting those needs protects the student's sense of trust, builds on what is already known and internalized, and instructs, with generalization into other situations as an underlying goal.

Braxton (1993) reported that people who are not allowed to be appropriately assertive resort to violence out of overwhelming feelings of powerlessness. Teaching students to be appropriately assertive is essential. Protecting the leadership status of a strong peer, rewarding that student's intent while shaping the roughness of his or her initial responses, and acknowledging the positive roles each student plays within the group helps students develop the necessary sense of trust and security.

8. Be aware of how individual needs affect group dynamics. Group members typically assume roles early in the establishment of the group dynamics. Redl (1966) made it clear that teachers must be aware of individual as well as group needs at all times. He used the term *marginal antiseptis* to signify the measurement standard by which any intervention is selected. Marginal antiseptis means that a given technique necessary for an individual must at the very least be harmless to the growth of the group and vice versa. Kounin (1977) described what he called the "ripple effect." Negative behaviors and attitudes can spread throughout a group with surprising speed. Awareness of the roles individuals play in the group and the signals of the group peer leader can be of great value in avoiding and diverting major disruptions.

9. Show empathy and unconditional regard at all times, but especially when students are in the midst of a crisis. Anthony should not have thrown the tray of food. Responding to his concern over his shirt, however, allowed him to get himself under control, see me as caring about his needs rather than only being interested in punishment, and eventually accept responsibility for his actions more gracefully.

   In a crisis, respond to students' needs first. Problem solving and consequences can only be managed effectively when students are calm and in control of themselves. Never forget the students' needs for concrete, consistently set limits. Once students are able to talk about the problem, it is imperative that they be held accountable for their choices. Anthony's growth and dignity could only be honored through the restitution involved in cleaning up the mess he had made.

10. Attend with extreme care to students' physiological as well as psychological needs. Have extra clothing, food, and drink available. Make washable pillows to use when students sit on the floor. Keep bandages, hand lotion, and soap available. Much of the acting out behavior reflects what Driekurs and colleagues (1982) referred to as a need for power or attention. Attempt to give as little emotional response as possible to inappropriate behavior. Make responses to appropriate behavior obviously animated and positive.

   Students will often respond to an affective bulletin board. Written recognition of their accomplishments throughout the days and weeks reinforces the teacher's role of benevolence and the students' needs for power and attention.

   The cafeteria problem is replayed again in the next anecdote. Typical Stage Two behaviors are illustrated along with the shift in the teacher's role from benevolent dictator to director.

Anthony stands up and bellows, "What's up, chump? Don't start your crap in here."

At this point, I intervene. "Anthony, have a seat. You're absolutely right. We don't need to have a problem here. Trina, what's wrong?"

"He did it again. The little shit did it again!"

"No, I didn't. She's lying."

"Carl, I'm talking with Trina right now. You'll get your turn in a minute. What did he do, Trina?"

"He spit a huge lugie right in my food."

"Let me see your tray." There was no evidence of saliva or phlegm on her tray. Carl's comment that he had done it again, however, led me to believe that he had done something. "OK, Carl, it's your turn. What did you do?"

"Nothing. I was just sitting here eating."

"What did you mean when you said, 'I did it again'?"

"I didn't say that."

"I heard you."

"Yeah. We did too." Anthony joins the conversation. "Why don't you just knock it off? You're not cool."

Carl knows that he is no match for Anthony. The rest of the group is either nonverbally agreeing with Anthony or not giving Carl eye contact.

"Oh, for Pete's sake! You can't take a joke at all!"

"OK, Carl. What's the joke?" I know what happened. It's important to finish the process with Carl, Trina, and the group. Taking Carl out of the situation too soon does not allow him to get adequate feedback from his peers.

"I was just playing."

"Trina, Anthony, and the others have made it clear to you before that they don't appreciate this kind of playing."

"So, that's their problem."

"No. It's yours now. The last time this happened, we had a group discussion. Do you remember what the group decided?"

"No." Carl shoots a look of defiance in my direction but carefully avoids eye contact with his peers.

"The group decided that it would be appropriate for people who spit or even pretend to spit on another's food to purchase that person a lunch, apologize, and be restricted from the cafeteria for 2 days."

Carl begins to escalate verbally and is escorted back to the classroom by Ms. Haines. Trina gets another tray. The class goes on with its usual routine. Anthony and Trina receive extra activity time for handling Carl's problem appropriately. The whole group earns extra bonus points toward items of their choice in the classroom store for not encouraging the escalation of the problem.

The teacher's role has shifted slightly. A discussion of critical needs and techniques necessary for successful group management during Stage Two is developed in the following section.

STAGE TWO: DIRECTOR

The teacher moves from benevolent dictator to director during Stage Two. The group members usually have enough trust in each other and the teacher to allow individuals to have their problems in isolation. A routine has been established for problem solving. Behavior modification techniques have provided a reliable system of recognition and reward for positive choices and consequences for inappropriate choices. The teacher can be more direct in problem-solving situations.

During Stage One, many problems are processed individually with the teacher to avoid further disruption of the group. Communication is between one student and one adult at a time. When the group moves into Stage Two, students begin to benefit from feedback from their peers, group problem-solving sessions, and group decision-making techniques designed to teach them the skills necessary for internal control of their choices. Communication still flows between one student and one adult at a time. The difference during Stage Two is that the rest of the group can and should be present to hear as well as to give feedback. The teacher directs the pace, quality, and quantity of information as the group participates in the problem-solving or decision-making process. Demands on the group must be monitored carefully and increased very gradually. Practical ways to enhance this growth include the following:

1. Establish a procedure for group problem solving. When problems arise that tend to affect all or most group members, take the class through predetermined and previously taught steps. Teach the steps using hypothetical problems initially. Attempting to teach problem-solving steps for the first time in the midst of a real group crisis would only invite disaster. Keep ground rules and steps simple. Tell students that everyone will be allowed to speak. Each person must state in specific, appropriate terms what he or she directly said, heard, or felt. Only one person talks at a time. No one is to speak for another group member, use name calling or profanity, or attempt to assign blame or motives to anyone else. Students who forget these guidelines will be reminded. If they are unwilling or unable to participate under these terms, they will be removed from the discussion.

   Problem-solving steps can be printed on chart paper, an overhead transparency, or the chalkboard. The steps for group problem solving are similar to the questions on the Think Sheet:

   Step 1. Define the problem.
       a. Actions
       b. Emotions

   Step 2. Determine the time, place, and people involved.

   Step 3. Brainstorm and list alternative actions.

   Step 4. Determine consequences for alternative actions.

   Step 5. Select the best alternative.

   Step 6. Check it out.

   Step 7. Evaluate.

   It is helpful to keep the completed chart or overhead transparency so the group can refer to the ideas generated during the reevaluation.

   Although the teacher directs this activity very carefully, it encourages movement from external to internal controls by placing the responsibility for thinking through problems and possible solutions on the group.

2. Set group goals that encourage a shift from "What's in it for me?" to "How can we accomplish this together?" Setting group goals followed by group rewards for reaching those goals focuses energy on making positive choices. This strategy can also help students save face during the awkward transition from earning attention and status through negative behavior to positive self-assertion and power.

   Group punishments are not appropriate or helpful. Administering a group punishment sets up a no-win situation for everyone. Cooperative group members feel unappreciated or betrayed. Uncooperative group members use the negative feelings in the group to undermine the teacher's authority.

   Make group goals small and attainable at first to build confidence through success. Gradually increase the complexity and difficulty level of the group goals as the group is ready. Engage the group members in setting goals and criteria to be reached.

On a day that the group is doing well, for instance, announce that 10 extra minutes of activity time will be awarded if all morning work is completed on time. Or make a thermometer for recording the number of homework assignments returned each day. Have a group meeting to discuss the total number of assignments completed and returned as well as the reward. The class might decide that a total of 50 assignments completed and returned would result in a popcorn and soda social.

The affective bulletin board idea described in the section on Stage One functioning can be expanded to include group goals. Paper chains representing intermediate steps to goal attainment can be used to reinforce the relationship between individual achievement and group functioning as well. Students need and benefit from concrete examples of the power each individual contributes to the well-being of the total group.

3. Teach decision-making skills. Allow the group to use them. Students need to know what is under their control and what is not. Do not confuse them. When they do have a choice, however, teach them skills for peaceful resolution. Initially the teacher may give the group two choices and hold a simple vote to determine the action taken. As time goes on, the group can be taught to generate ideas, debate issues to narrow the field of choices based on group-determined criteria, and make a final decision. Once again, the trick is to move the group slowly from simple voting to real negotiation by directly teaching communication and decision-making skills.

4. Encourage the group's peer leader to be more vocal when he or she is able to be positive. Positive peer pressure is invaluable.

5. Allow students to begin to work as partners. Peer tutoring can be a wonderful strategy for developing social-emotional as well as academic competence. Students in classes for EBD need direct instruction in how to accomplish this prerequisite task before they can complete independent and age-appropriate cooperative learning activities successfully. Research on and practical application of this strategy are explained fully in Chapter 5.

As the group develops a sense of belonging and the majority of group members begin to regularly self-monitor and exhibit self-control, Stage Three functioning emerges. The third and final replay of the cafeteria incident illustrates typical Stage Three behaviors and the corresponding role of the teacher.

"Carl, get out of my face." Trina looks and sounds irritated but keeps her voice at an appropriate volume for the situation.

Carl begins to giggle and slap his thigh. Trina, Jo, Tory, and Ann slide to the far end of the table and resume their discussion of the new spring styles while Anthony, Mark, and Carlos are debating the odds that their favorite players will be selected in the first draft. I make a mental note to call Carl's mother, and quietly thank Trina for moving away from him. Trina nods and keeps on talking.

STAGE THREE: ARBITRATOR

More often than not, students can resolve issues on their own at this stage. The teacher's role shifts from director to arbitrator. When the group does need adult intervention, decisions can be finalized by the group with supportive assistance from the teacher to ensure that rules and procedures are honored by every group member for the benefit of all.

Students in regular education settings encounter conflicts with peers frequently. They learn to maneuver difficult social situations through experience and practice. Due to smaller class sizes and partial, if not total, separation of their classes from the mainstream, students with EBD have fewer opportunities to learn and practice a variety of age-appropriate peer negotiation skills. This hinders the development of successful strategies. As soon as a group begins to exhibit a safe level of self-control, the teacher must control his or her impulse to intervene. Mastery and generalization to other settings cannot occur with skills that continually require external management.

TEACHERS' INDIVIDUAL STYLES

To respond to the changing needs of the group, the teacher must be capable of high degrees of empathy and self-efficacy. Teachers who are more naturally inclined to be nurturing, understanding, and accepting of divergence will find the Stage One role of benevolent dictator uncomfortable. Strict adherence to behavior modification techniques can leave a more psychodynamically oriented educator feeling cold and uncaring. On the other hand, the teacher who is very comfortable with a clinical behavior modification approach that relies heavily on teacher-controlled contingencies may feel uneasy with the transfer of power and control to the group during Stage Two and Stage Three.

The most natural action on the part of the teacher may not be the most appropriate one in response to group needs at a particular time. The self-administered checklist on pages 26–27 can be used to help teachers become aware of natural tendencies with respect to behavior management. A resource list follows to assist teachers in locating additional materials that might support and enhance personal style. It is important to respect personal beliefs and philosophies in the planning and execution of behavior management.

IT WORKS FOR ME!

This is a forced-choice self-evaluation tool to assist teachers with the selection of classroom management strategies. There are no right or wrong answers. On most items, most teachers would find both choices to be valid at some level. Select the sentence from each of the paired items that would be most comfortable for you as a teacher.

1. a. Children need to learn to behave within socially accepted boundaries.
   b. Children need to be allowed to develop at their own rates.

2. a. Teachers have a responsibility to help students understand the reasons for rules and to live within them.
   b. Teachers have a responsibility to establish and enforce rules.

3. a. Punishment is not necessary or helpful in encouraging social-emotional development. It focuses the child on feelings of anger or guilt instead of an understanding of himself or herself and the situation.
   b. Punishment is a last resort, but it is necessary at times to decrease or extinguish certain behaviors.

4. a. Rewards increase the likelihood that a behavior will be repeated and are very useful in teaching appropriate social skills.
   b. Relationships are important factors in social-emotional development and lay the groundwork for successful attainment of socially acceptable behavior.

5. a. Self-efficacy is learned through physiological responses to situations, feedback from others, objective data, and personal beliefs.
   b. Self-esteem develops through unconditional acceptance, attainment and maintenance of relationships, and successful mastery of development milestones.

6. a. The most important trait a teacher could exhibit would be an ability to unconditionally accept a student as a valued person. Behavior is separated from a sense of self-worth.
   b. The most important trait a teacher could exhibit would be consistency in response to desirable and undesirable behaviors.

7. a. Because many behaviors are developmental in nature, teachers must provide a supportive and enriching environment that fosters growth.
   b. Because behavior is learned, teachers must learn to modify student behaviors by ignoring, rewarding, and punishing.

8. a. Students must have their basic needs met in order to work and learn most efficiently.
   b. Students must receive a reward of some type, either tangible or intangible, in order to continue to work.

9. a. Instruction needs to be presented in small, easily understood increments to increase success and reduce the likelihood of practicing errors.
   b. Instruction needs to involve the whole student. Skills learned in isolation have less meaning.

10. a. Students need to know consequences, both positive and negative, in order to learn appropriate behavior.
    b. Students need acceptance from caring adults and an understanding of themselves and others in order to attain and maintain appropriate relationships.

Source: *Back Off, Cool Down, Try Again*, Sylvia Rockwell, 1995, Reston, VA: The Council for Exceptional Children.

Find your score by adding the numbers that correspond to each of your choices.

1. a – 1	4. a – 1	7. a – 5	9. a – 1
b – 5	b – 5	b – 1	b – 5
2. a – 5	5. a – 1	8. a – 5	10. a – 1
b – 1	b – 5	b – 1	b – 5
3. a – 5	6. a – 5		
b – 1	b – 1	YOUR TOTAL _____	

Items in "It Works for Me!" are taken from various behavioral and developmental intervention approaches. To select strategies that are most compatible with their philosophies, teachers should combine an analysis of personal beliefs with corresponding material available for classroom use. The following explanation of total scores will assist teachers in selecting materials that are most appropriate to their needs and philosophies.

Total Score	*Philosophical Base and Materials*
10–23	**Strongly Behavioral** *Assertive Discipline* *Teacher Effectiveness Training* *Applied Behavior Analysis for Teachers*
24–37	**Eclectic/Cognitive Behavioral** *The Prepare Curriculum* *Thinking, Feeling, Behaving* *Positive Action*
38–50	**Strongly Developmental** *DUSO* *Cooperative Discipline* *Positive Discipline*

ADDITIONAL RESOURCES

Charles, C. M. (1992). *Building Classroom Discipline*

DeBruyn, R. L. & Larson, J. L. (1984). *You Can Handle Them All*

Sprick, R. (1981). *The Solution Book*

Developmental programs for individuals are outlined in detail in Swap (1974); Dryngelson (1992); and Wood, Combs, Gunn, and Weller (1986). Readers who want further reading in the development of therapeutic programming for individual students will find a wealth of information in those three sources.

Now that individual development and its impact on group dynamics have been examined with respect to the teacher's changing role through expected group developmental stages, Chapter 4 will explore the differences between individual and group management strategies. The guiding strategies in terms of selection and use will also be examined.

Individual Versus Group Management

The key to everything is patience. You get the chicken by hatching the egg, not by smashing it.
—A. H. Glasow

Earlier, Carl had a problem with inappropriate pranks in the cafeteria. When he enters the time out area, the following events occur.

"Carl," Ms. Cortez directs, "Please sit here. You have a problem-solving sheet to complete before we talk."

"Up yours, Bitch!" Carl responds.

"You know the rules in here, Carl. One warning is all you get. This is it."

"I didn't do nothing. Why do I have to do a problem-solving sheet?" Carl whines.

"Mrs. Rockwell says that you pretended to spit on Trina's food."

"Yeah. So?"

"So, the problem started with that behavior and got bigger. A problem-solving sheet will help you decide on a better plan for the future."

"It's not my problem if Trina can't take a joke."

"Has she asked you before not to joke with her that way?"

"Yeah, but . . . ."

"No buts, Carl. It's your problem if you keep doing something that gets you sent here. Complete the problem solving sheet and then we'll talk."

"OK, OK. Geez . . . What a rip!"

Although there may be organic reasons for inappropriate behavior including illness, chemical imbalances in the brain, neurological dysfunction, or allergic reactions, teachers must understand the psychological motivations that drive thought and behavior patterns if they are to select and execute effective behavior management strategies. Carl is on medication for attention deficit with hyperactivity disorder (ADHD). The medication helps him focus his attention and appear less hyperactive, but it does not satisfy his need for attention. Carl's problem-solving sheet, interview, and individual behavior plan will address his need for attention by helping him learn new, more appropriate ways to attract and maintain peer relationships. Old, less appropriate behaviors will result in consequences such as removal from the cafeteria, loss of privileges, or time out. In planning for behavioral change it is essential to address the motivation for the inappropriate behavior; teach and provide practice in the new behaviors; and punish old behaviors. Failure to attend to all three steps in the behavior change process will result in failure to reach the desired outcome.

Carl's problem-solving sheet looked like the one shown on page 31.

The following interview took place immediately following Carl's completion of time out and the problem-solving form.

"OK, Carl. What have you learned?"

"That Trina can't take a joke."

"According to your problem-solving sheet, Trina has the problem."

"Yeah."

"So why are you here?"

"'Cause I didn't know that Trina had a problem."

"OK, Carl. It's time to get serious. Here's a new problem-solving sheet. Let's try this again. What was *your* behavior during the problem that started in the cafeteria?"

"I pretended to spit on Trina's food."

"Write that. Now, what could you have done to get Trina's attention instead of pretending to spit on her food?"

"Well, I guess I could have asked her something."

"Like what?"

"I don't know. Like . . . like what she thought of the dorky notes that that little suck-up, Ann, always gives to Mrs. Rockwell."

"What would happen if you asked a question like that?"

"Everyone would laugh."

"Everyone?"

"No. Goof Ball, Ann, would just stare out the window and Mrs. Rockwell would say, 'Carl, rephrase. Name calling is inappropriate.'" [This last comment was made in a high, sing-song voice.]

"OK, so try again. How could you get Trina's attention without getting into a problem?"

DECISION-MAKING SHEET

Name _____ Carl _____

Date _____

1. What was happening before the problem occurred? _____
   _____ I was eating. _____
   _____

2. What was your behavior when the problem began? _____
   _____ Fine _____
   _____

3. How did you feel? _____ Fine _____

4. What other things could you have done? Name at least four that would have been
   more appropriate. _____
   _____ nothing _____

   _____ Trina is stupid. _____
   _____

5. Which one of the four behaviors you listed in question 4 would you like best?
   _____ nothing _____

   Why would your prefer to do that? _____
   _____ nothing _____

   What would you have earned if you had chosen that behavior instead of the one you
   described in question 2? _____
   _____ nothing _____

6. What has the problem behavior earned for you? _____
   _____ nothing _____

7. How are you feeling now? _____ Fine _____
   _____

8. Did you make any good decisions in spite of the problem? What were they?
   _____
   _____

9. What can you do now to help yourself have a good day? _____
   _____
   _____

"Geez, man. I already told you guys. I don't have a problem. Everyone's so damned serious around here. People can't even laugh. This place is like a prison."

"So you like people spitting in your food?"

"No! But I didn't spit in the little witch's food. I just pretended! God have mercy! What does it take to get you freaks to understand?"

"I heard you. You just pretended to spit. You also admitted that Trina had asked you not to do this. Her request is a reasonable one. The problem to be solved here is how to get Trina's attention without ending up in time out."

"Can I leave?"

"No. We're not done."

"I did my time and completed the stupid problem-solving sheet. I'm done. You can finish without me."

"No, Carl. Your problem-solving sheet is incomplete. And, because this problem has happened before and it resulted in physical aggression this time, we also have a behavior plan to do. So I suggest that you get down to business here."

"Fuck this shit, man! I ain't done nothing. This is crap!"

"I understand that you're angry and want to leave. I'll give you 10 minutes to cool off. When the 10 minutes are up, we'll try again. You control how long you need to be here by how long it takes you to complete your time and paperwork."

Carl eventually completes his time, the problem-solving sheet, and the behavior plan (contract). Copies are made. Carl keeps one copy of each paper. Mrs. Rockwell gets a copy. Ms. Cortez keeps one. One is sent to Carl's mother. The behavior plan is monitored and updated every 2 to 3 weeks. A copy of Carl's second problem-solving sheet and a copy of the first behavior plan are provided on pages 33 and 34. Blank copies of each can be found in the Appendix.

Although many teachers and administrators believe that students in special education classes should have individualized behavior plans, it has been my experience that group planning is essential to the success of individuals within the group setting. A carefully developed group plan that allows for individual needs within the context of the group preserves the dual goals of affective development. Students in classrooms for EBD need a balance of self-management skills and relationship-building skills. Individual and group awareness must be kept in healthy perspective.

Individual behavior plans may become necessary occasionally. Carl's cafeteria behavior, for example, had great potential for escalation into dangerous acting out by others. Carl was the only one in the group exhibiting that particular behavior. The group plan was not meeting Carl's needs sufficiently. Under those conditions, a short-term individualized behavior plan is warranted. Teachers attempting to use individual behavior plans should consider the following points (see page 35):

DECISION-MAKING SHEET

Name _____Carl_____

Date _____

1. **What was happening before the problem occurred?** _____
   _____I was eating._____
   _____

2. **What was your behavior when the problem began?** _____
   _____I was just teasing._____
   _____

3. **How did you feel?** _____like having a good time_____

4. **What other things could you have done? Name at least four that would have been more appropriate.** _____
   _____1) tell a joke_____
   _____2) tease someone who has a sense of humor_____
   _____3) be quiet_____
   _____4) eat_____

5. **Which one of the four behaviors you listed in question 4 would you like best?**
   _____tell a joke_____

   Why would your prefer to do that? _____
   _____I like to make people laugh._____

   What would you have earned if you had chosen that behavior instead of the one you described in question 2? _____
   _____a good time_____

6. **What has the problem behavior earned for you?** _____
   _____Time Out_____

7. **How are you feeling now?** _____mad_____
   _____

8. **Did you make any good decisions in spite of the problem? What were they?**
   _____Yes. I talked with the behavior specialist._____
   _____

9. **What can you do now to help yourself have a good day?** _____
   ___Follow directions_____
   _____

CONTRACT

1. Problem Behaviors

Pretending to spit on classmate's food.

2. Desired Behavior

Enjoy eating with the class.

3. Punishments

— Time Out

— Pay for a new lunch for the person offended

— Loss of cafeteria privileges for a week

4. Rewards

Eat with the class.

Time with a staff member of choice

Pass to eat with another class

Rewards are contingent upon appropriate completion of punishments and continued compliance in the cafeteria..

5. Signatures

Student *Carl Johnson*

Teacher *Sylvia Rockwell*

Any Other Staff Member(s) Involved *Juanita Cortez*

1. Especially during Stage One development, the group has many fears surrounding issues of fairness. For this reason, it is important not to offer an individual a reward that could not be offered to everyone. The other students may not ask for the specific item or privilege after the first day or two. They do need the reassurance, however, that they will not be left out or treated unfairly.

2. Individual behavior plans should address the motivation for the target behavior by offering rewards that meet the need(s) motivating the misbehavior. A student who acts out to get attention needs to be given appropriate outlets for expressing this need. The likelihood that students with EBD will develop appropriate alternative behaviors on their own is slim. Attempting to extinguish one behavior without replacing it with another, more appropriate behavior leads to additional problems.

3. Individual behavior plans take time, energy, and attention from group instruction and management. Having students on individual plans can fragment efforts to pull the class together unless individual plans are kept simple and compatible with the group management strategies already in place. For example, a student who needs it can receive more frequent and tangible forms of attention with the same tokens, bonus points, or earned activity time the group plan utilizes. Individual reinforcement schedules can be modified. Items and activities used as rewards can be targeted to specifically meet individuals' needs. Consequences or punishments can be extended to include restitution, overcorrection, or positive practice. However, individual modifications should never give one student an advantage over the others in terms of greater rewards or lesser consequences for the same behaviors. To do that invites the fury and distrust of the group while escalating negative behaviors.

   Offering one student more privileges and fewer consequences for the same behaviors others in the group exhibit sends a negative message to the student receiving special treatment as well. The student who is treated in a deferential way often interprets such treatment as a lack of trust in his or her ability to do better. Students tend to live up or down to teacher expectations. Unless a student is clearly capable of less than his or her classmates, it is best to make subtle modifications and convey an expectation that all group members will live up to group standards.

4. Individual needs can be incorporated in the following ways:

   (a) Adjust the tone of voice used to the need of the student being addressed. Some students respond best to a firm, quiet voice; others need a more soothing tone.

   (b) Adjust the timing of the responses and movement through the classroom interventions to meet students' needs. Some students respond best to a quick count of three when a direction is given; others would respond to such a count by refusing to comply. To avoid a power struggle, the teacher can present the student with choices and set a time limit for the student to decide.

   (c) Assign students jobs in the classroom that meet their individual needs. A hyperactive student may need to move around periodically. Give that student errands to run. Time these errands to help the student avoid problems. Another student may need a great deal of personal attention. Allow that student to be an assistant to the classroom aide or another adult in the school. Students who feel inadequate in academic areas often get a boost from helping younger students.

(d)   When problem solving, adjust the pace and tone to the needs of individuals. Some students benefit from an explanation of teacher motives and attempts to encourage insight such as in the discussion with Jo in Chapter 1. Other students respond best to a quick, firm statement of limits and choices.

Understanding the individual needs of each student allows the teacher to respond appropriately to each one while preserving the overall group management structure. Chapter 5 will address effective group management strategies.

Group Management Strategies

You can build a throne with bayonets; but you can't sit on it for long.—Boris Yeltsin

Carl's cafeteria problem had implications for the whole group. Failing to deal effectively with Carl would undermine the group's need to feel protected. The teacher would only be given the status of an authority if the ability to lead and protect the group were maintained. The group was increasingly able to tolerate Carl's cafeteria antics without becoming volatile because an overall structure existed to support and encourage appropriate behavior.

Let's look at a common classroom scenario that involves the whole group. As the events unfold, elements of effective group planning are illustrated. A discussion of each component will follow the anecdote.

"All right, class. Let's get started. Raise your hand if you have your point card."

"Jo, Mark, Carl, Ann, Tory, and Carlos, you earned three stars."

Ms. Haines collects signed point cards from the previous day and totals the new balances. Trina, Tory, and Anthony will have a 0 balance until their point cards are signed by a parent and returned.

"How many of you have your homework?" No one responds initially. "Remember, it's worth two bonus point stars and a grade in the grade book. It also counts as a sign-off toward the Friday activity." Slowly Ann, Jo, and Carlos raise their hands. As Ms. Haines moves around the room to collect the homework and sign off on their work sign-off sheets, the others start to snicker and make rude comments.

"Shut up, you bunch of snot-sucking assholes before I bust you up!" Jo shouts.

At this remark, Tory, Trina, Carl, and Mark howl with laughter. Carl falls on the floor laughing and kicks his legs in the air. Mark offers to let Jo take her best shot.

Ann and Anthony look on slightly amused. In less than 60 seconds, a quiet classroom has erupted into a potential riot scene.

"Jo, you have to the count of three to sit." I say this in a firm, controlled voice as I move between Jo and Mark. It is important to achieve three goals at this point: (1) to keep both students in sight; (2) to attempt to break the eye contact between Jo and Mark; and (3) to maintain a nonthreatening stance while providing support through proximity to the students in distress.

"Stay away from me, Bitch. He asked for it. He's going to get it!" Jo begins to move in Mark's direction. I move toward Mark and begin to count.

"One . . . Jo, is Mark's remark worth the field trip, Friday activity, and an extra art period this afternoon?" Jo stops moving toward Mark and looks at me.

"Why are you on his side?"

"I'm not on anyone's side. I want you to earn the activities you've been looking forward to. I'll talk with Mark if you'll take a seat."

Jo glares at Mark, shows him her middle finger, and moves to cool off.

"Hell, no! HELL, NO! She's not getting away with that now." Mark's mood turns from playful threats to real anger. Carl is still laughing but takes his cue to at least get off the floor. Anthony steps in before I can speak.

"Just sit down, man."

"Didn't you see what she did?"

"Yeah, I saw. She's a girl. What does she know?"

"Don't start with us girls, punk!" Trina shouts at Anthony.

It is clear that this is not going to be resolved easily. The problems keep bouncing from one person to another. Getting people quiet and under control is the first priority.

As usual, Ann has maintained a passive stance throughout mounting distress within the group. Carl has stopped laughing momentarily to settle into a comfortable viewing position. I quickly place "No Homework" coupons on Ann's and Carl's desks and thank them for being quiet. Ann had earned bonus stars on the chalkboard prior to this. The promise of an opportunity to use the stars to purchase a special snack at midmorning follows. With this cue, Anthony shrugs his shoulders at Mark and faces forward. One by one, the class begins the independent boardwork assignment designed to focus and structure this initial period of the day. As they get to work, I assign bonus stars and award Anthony a "No Homework" coupon for attempting to stop Mark from having a problem. I then conference with Jo and Mark. They both have consequences for threatening. The others earn varying amounts of zeroes for their parts in encouraging the spread of the problem by laughing.

Once control is regained, a group affective lesson is conducted to identify the problem and future solutions. The class suggests that a box be provided for homework and point cards. Students could put their items in the box without being noticed. Credit would be quietly recorded on their point cards and work sign-off sheets. No one would need to feel embarrassed about following the teacher's directions in front of others.

I applaud their creative problem solving and agree to follow through on their suggestion. I also add laughing at people to the category of name calling. Name calling carries with it the penalty of a zero on the point card, 5 minutes in cool off, and rephrasing the rude comment before earning points on a first offense. A second offense equals 15 minutes in in-class suspension with four zeroes on the point card, and rephrasing. A third offense requires the student to fill out a Think Sheet, spend 30 minutes in in-class suspension, earn eight zeroes, and rephrase.

Trina, Jo, and Carl think I am stupid to require a consequence for laughing. I explain that appropriate laughter is encouraged. Making fun of people, however, does not qualify as an appropriate use of laughter. Their pouting faces tell me that they will be testing me on this. By this time, the class is calm and ready to proceed with its usual routine.

Establishing effective behavior management strategies requires balancing the following four major elements: (1) the teacher, (2) the conditions, (3) the consequences, and (4) the curriculum (Guetzloe [n.d.a.], Kounin [1977], Hewett & Taylor [1980]). The absence or underdevelopment of any one of the four major elements will significantly weaken the effectiveness of each of the others. Group behavior management requires a complex, well-structured web of consequences, rewards, verbal intervention strategies, and proactive environmental and academic planning strategies, as well as high degrees of teacher empathy, self-efficacy, and flexibility.

This chapter's opening quote emphasizes the importance of remembering to accentuate the positive when working with students in classes for EBD. Threatening already distressed students with consequences will only escalate their anger, fear, and distrust. The most natural reactions to threats include fighting or running. Neither reaction would be appropriate, effective, or safe when working with emotionally labile groups.

THE TEACHER

The following characteristics of effective behavior managers will be supported by practical suggestions for use in the classroom. Effective behavior managers:

1. Respect their own strengths and weaknesses as seriously as those of their students.

2. Understand that social-emotional growth is a never-ending process.

3. Clearly communicate rules, goals, and expectations.

4. Respond to behaviors consistently and predictably.

5. Discriminate between issues of responsibility and problem ownership.

6. Exhibit high degrees of empathy and self-efficacy.

Kounin (1977) described many of the behaviors teachers exhibit that contribute to classroom management. Having materials organized, using a pleasant tone of voice, being aware of multiple elements of group functioning simultaneously, and being able to anticipate possible problems and react quickly to avoid them are essential teacher skills. According to Allinder (1993), high levels of self-efficacy have a positive effect on behavior management as well as academic achievement. Teachers who exhibit high levels of self-efficacy use more positive reinforcement, prefer to work with the whole group, and persist with students who are experiencing difficulty rather than ignoring or giving up on them. The ability to be empathetic has also been shown by Morgan and Reinhart (1991) to be associated with student success. Empathetic teachers report experiencing less stress and exhibit the following qualities:

1. Warm
2. Caring
3. Affectionate
4. Friendly (smiles frequently)
5. Soft-spoken
6. Calm
7. Relaxed
8. Humorous
9. Analytical of behavior and motives
10. Able to predict how another will act
11. Able to sympathize
12. Not easily incited to express anger
13. Not easily depressed under difficult circumstances
14. Able to subordinate their own needs and feelings for another's benefit
15. Spontaneous
16. Balanced in feelings of self-worth and self-regard
17. Encouraging
18. Inspiring
19. Motivating
20. Adaptable to the needs of others
21. Altruistic (desire to make a personal contribution)
22. Able to give positive verbal and nonverbal feedback
23. Conscientious in attending to students' needs
24. A person who does not need to be the center of attention
25. A person who makes others centrally involved
26. A person who is independent and creative
27. Totally accepting of individual differences but does not focus on deviance
28. A highly intuitive and feeling being
29. A person who does not feel a great need to control all people and events

(Morgan & Reinhart, 1991, pp. 199–200)

To remain empathetic and self-confident, a teacher must understand social-emotional growth and accept a responsible role in facilitating that growth without owning the student's problems. After a tough day, it is easy to blame either the students or yourself. Neither approach will work for long; either one will lead to burnout. It is much more productive to analyze the situations that occurred. Who did what? Could any of the problems have been avoided? How? What should be done in the future? After carefully sorting out the components that are controllable from the ones that are beyond control, make the necessary adaptations and put the energy and time left into what can be done. Focusing yourself and the students on what is possible is much more effective than assigning blame. Do not accept blame for problems you could not have controlled. Do make adjustments and even apologize for honest mistakes.

Social-emotional growth is a lifelong process. Remembering that students will need multiple experiences to master social-emotional issues just as they need multiple experiences to learn academic material makes the process more of an adventure and less of a chore. It also helps to remember that teachers are involved in their own process of social-emotional growth. Accepting our students is easier when we are accepting of ourselves.

The list of characteristics of empathetic teachers from Morgan and Reinhart's (1991) research provides a checklist of qualities to examine. No one person could realistically be expected to exhibit all 29 characteristics consistently. However, a model that is supported by research as being most effective gives us a standard by which to measure our own progress and set personal goals. The teacher is only one component in the success of the growth and education of a group. The conditions surrounding students and teachers need examination as well.

THE CONDITIONS

Conditions, according to Hewett and Taylor (1980), include the physical environment as well as elements of scheduling, special events, the ratio of students to adults, the number and nature of interruptions, and the general atmosphere of the school and the community. Ecological factors can often be the easiest to manipulate. If the class is easily overstimulated by whole group activities in the beginning, keep these periods brief. Have nonthreatening independent assignments and activities available. Alternate whole group and individual activity periods throughout the day. Be especially aware of the need for self-structuring, quiet activities after lunch and physical education. Gradually increase the length of the whole group activities as the class is able to successfully participate in them.

Other items to consider would include the list shown in Figure 5.1, compiled by Guetzloe (n.d.a).

THE CONSEQUENCES

Consequences include rewards for compliance and punishments for noncompliance. Establishing a safe and trustworthy classroom climate requires a healthy mixture of expectations, standards, and consequences for meeting or failing to meet those expectations and standards.

FIGURE 5.1

CLASSROOM ARRANGEMENT CHECKLIST

Door

    Clearly marked

    Envelope, pad, pencil, for messages

    Space inside for lining up

Walls

    Displays at students' eye level

    Displays offer classroom information, instruction, and entertainment

    Displays students' work and art

    Schedules posted, kept current, and in blocks of time that do not exceed 30 minutes

    Broken or malfunctioning outlets have been reported

    Chipped or blemished walls have been reported

    Some open space is available

Furniture

    Each student's desk is of appropriate size

    Each child has his or her own assigned seat

    Each student's desk is organized for easy access to materials

    Each student has adequate space

    Desks are arranged so each child can see and participate in seatwork

    Desks are arranged so that each student can observe the teacher, presentations, and the chalkboard

    There is a quiet or "time out" area

    There are study carrels, "offices," or dividers for distraction-free space

Equipment and Materials

    Materials and equipment are stored in a logical order and place

    Materials and equipment are readily available

    Inventory sheet is maintained for all materials

    Materials and supplies can be stored behind closed doors

    Locked storage is available

    Materials and supplies are stored close to area of use

Student Records

    Student records are kept in a convenient place

    Student records are orderly

Comfort

    Temperature control is adequate

    Lighting is adequate

Guetzloe, E. C. (n.d.a), from a handout for class and presentations.

Source: *Back Off, Cool Down, Try Again*, Sylvia Rockwell, 1995, Reston, VA: The Council for Exceptional Children.

Rules, according to Alberto and Troutman (1982), should be specific, few in number, and logical in relation to consequences. Specific rules state expectations in observable, behavioral terms. Instead of "Respect others," the rule might state, "Keep hands, feet, and other objects to yourself." Students will be more successful if the number of rules is kept to five or fewer. Concentrating on the group's most expedient issues keeps students focused.

Making consequences logical strengthens the learning process and helps prevent the development of manipulative behaviors. For instance, if a student is sent to time out for failing to complete an assignment, he or she may learn to be noncompliant to avoid doing unpleasant tasks. If the consequence for failing to complete work is using a desired activity period for completing unfinished work, the consequence strengthens the desired learning outcome without encouraging further avoidance behaviors.

Rewards are most effective when they reinforce the logical aspects of learning as well. Students who complete work on time and like to play basketball can be awarded time to go outside for that activity based on the fact that using time wisely earlier in the day provided time in the schedule for other, more desirable activities. This step in the process may take a few months. Tangible, immediate rewards may be needed in the beginning. As soon as students are ready, however, social and age-appropriate activity reinforcers should be incorporated into the intricate web of consequences. Moving students from a dependency on external adult supervision and reinforcement to internal self-monitoring and rewarding is a slow process. The movement from a behavioral orientation of management in Stage One to teaching students prerequisite communication and problem-solving skills during Stage Two to authentic cooperative learning and cooperative disciplining strategies in Stage Three requires advance planning and teacher awareness.

Components of behavior modification and cooperative discipline must be merged and modified to meet the group's needs as growth occurs. The following information can be used to make decisions regarding behavior management in response to developmental indications.

STAGE ONE: ESTABLISHING LIMITS

Establish limits with clearly defined rules, consequences for noncompliance, and rewards for appropriate responses. Make students aware of their power of choice in deciding to earn either the consequences or the rewards. Make consequences instructional. Students need a clear understanding of the desired behavior. Consequences that require practicing the desired behavior are particularly effective. Consequences should also be hierarchical. Start with a verbal reminder and move in increments to the most severe intervention. The same holds true for rewards. Rewards that reinforce the desired behavior and increase in proportion to the difficulty of the targeted behavior are most successful.

Some steps in the hierarchy of consequences that have been helpful include the following:

1. Verbal warning.

2. Visual reminder on the chalkboard.

3. Cool off—a brief period in a carrel to focus on positive alternatives and remove the student from the source of frustration. (Points can be earned here.)

4. Point(s) not earned on point card.

5. In-class suspension (ICS)—a longer period in another carrel or isolated part of the classroom to focus on positive alternatives. (Points cannot be earned here.)

6. ICS with a Think Sheet—time in the carrel with a problem-solving form to be filled out. (Points cannot be earned.)

7. Time out—time in another classroom. (Students sit in an ICS carrel in another room and do not interact with other adults or students. If a behavior specialist is available, the student may sit with the behavior specialist. This is followed by ICS time to reinforce the importance of solving problems quickly to avoid longer consequences. No points are earned during time out or the ICS that follows.)

8. In-school suspension (ISS)—extended time in another room in the school. (Work is provided. A Think Sheet is required. No points are earned. ICS is required upon returning to class.)

9. Out-of-school suspension. This can be done as a formal suspension or a day of school exclusion. Behaviors that warrant such a consequence are serious. Students return to school with ISS and ICS time to do.

If students steal or destroy property, some type of restitution is useful. Working to pay off the debt, paying with classroom points earned, repairing or replacing the item(s), or bringing in money from home are possible options. Restitution strengthens the lessons of choice and responsibility that are being taught throughout the instructional, affective, and behavior management program.

The number of rewards available must exceed the number of consequences and move hierarchically in size and desirability as well as in developmental appropriateness from primary to secondary in nature. Emphasis on making appropriate choices and on the teacher's desire to provide ample opportunities for recognition of success helps to overcome the negatively charged beliefs students bring to the group. Rewards should be woven throughout the behavior management planning to support academic as well as social-emotional growth. Stressing on-task behaviors and academic accomplishments in the reward system can help students focus on what is desirable rather than on more negative choices.

In order for rewards to be meaningful, the behaviors that they are contingent on must be challenging without being overwhelming. Students will react negatively to being rewarded for behaviors that they consider to be beneath their abilities. Although food items and tangible trinkets may be necessary in the beginning, these should always be paired with rewards that encourage movement toward more age-appropriate, social reinforcers. Smiles, words of thanks or encouragement, recognition in the form of bulletin board announcements, and a personal recounting of success or progress through journal entries are examples of rewards that more mature students will respond to favorably.

A strict, fair, and consistent adherence to a behavior management program during Stage One lays a foundation for growth by establishing safety, trust, order, and structure. Nothing therapeutic can occur in chaos. Stage Two represents a transitional phase during which the group learns the skills necessary to effective interdependent functioning.

FIGURE 5.2

RULES, CONSEQUENCES, AND REWARDS

Rules

1. Remain in your assigned area.
2. Keep hands, feet, and other objects to yourself.
3. Complete tasks on time.
4. Use materials appropriately.
5. Raise your hand and wait to be recognized before talking.

Hierarchy of Consequences

1. Verbal warning.
2. Nonverbal reminder.
3. Zero earned on the point card.
4. Cool off.
5. In-class suspension.
6. In-class suspension with a Think Sheet.
7. Exclusion from class activities in a time out area followed by in-class suspension.
8. Exclusion from school.

Hierarchy of Rewards

1. Verbal praise.
2. Points earned on the point card.
3. Bonus points earned.
4. Tangible items earned.
5. Certificates.
6. Student of the Week or Turnaround Student of the Week.
7. Recognition in the school newsletter, on announcements, or on the affective bulletin board.
8. Activity period.
9. Special activity periods.
10. Visiting another class or staff member.
11. Classroom jobs.
12. Permission to run errands or have an on-site job in the cafeteria, media center, or office.
13. Peer tutoring in other classrooms with younger students.
14. Access to art materials, musical instruments, or computers.
15. Field trips and other community-based experiences.

Please note that the opportunities to be rewarded outnumber items in the list of consequences. It is important to stress this point with students. Attaching chart paper to the wall from the ceiling to the floor with a class-generated list of possible rewards is an enjoyable and useful exercise at the beginning of the term. Students need to see that while the teacher is prepared to deal with inappropriate behaviors, the emphasis for the year will be on learning and celebrating individual and group successes. Do not be afraid to be creative and resourceful in helping students compile a list of favored rewards. When our school acquired an ice machine, ice in a 2 gallon jug of water became a much appreciated reward for walking back to class in an orderly fashion. Those who did not want to comply with group rules still received water. Theirs came from the tap. Little things may not be of importance to adults. Let the students help guide assigning items to the list and ordering them.

Source: *Back Off, Cool Down, Try Again*, Sylvia Rockwell, 1995, Reston, VA: The Council for Exceptional Children.

STAGE TWO: ESTABLISHING PROCEDURES

During Stage Two, the group can benefit from the instruction and gradual application of communication and social skills required in group activities. Students often need to be taught to identify emotions. Even older students may not be aware of the physiological responses that accompany their emotions. Students commonly confuse their emotions and their bodies' reactions to emotions with behaviors. They are initially unable to separate feelings and actions. Anger and physical aggression, for example, may be synonymous as far as they are concerned. Teaching them to identify emotions, separate feelings from behaviors, and communicate wants and needs effectively are the major tasks during Stage Two.

All of the behavior management components established during Stage One limit setting must remain in place. The changes that occur in Stage Two are additive. In addition to externally managed consequences and rewards, the teacher actively instructs students in relaxation training, effective verbal and nonverbal communication strategies, decision-making procedures, and problem-solving skills. The group's assistance is enlisted in developing solutions to group problems. A powerful example of this group management technique in action is illustrated by an experience with an intermediate level elementary class. One of the boys named Steve had a problem with encopresis. He refused to change his clothes when he had an accident because he thought the class would know. The class knew anyway because of the odor. Name calling, arguing, and power struggles continued. Talking with the class when Steve was not present did not help. In spite of my explanations, they believed that he made them miserable deliberately. Talking with Steve alone did not help. He believed that the others hated him and would not accept him under any conditions. This was no longer one student's problem. It was affecting the whole group.

With a great deal of reassurance, I finally convinced Steve to allow the class to problem solve with him. I laid the ground rules before we started by stating the following procedural guidelines:

1. No name calling or rude comments would be tolerated.

2. Each person would have an opportunity to speak.

3. Each person could speak only for himself or herself.

4. Each person had a responsibility as a group member to be honest.

Steve sat in a chair in front of the class. I stood behind him with my hand on his shoulder to reassure him of my support and to emphasize to the group that he was to be treated respectfully. Steve was allowed to speak first. I encouraged him to explain the medical facts related to his condition. The other students' facial expressions, tone of voice, and body language changed from ridicule and amusement to genuine concern as Steve talked. Steve had had many medical problems in his short life. I then asked Steve to tell the class how he felt when they made fun of him or refused to sit next to him. He was reminded (as were his classmates) to use "I" statements as taught in lessons taken from Canfield's (1986) *Self-Esteem in the Classroom*. He responded with feelings of sadness, embarrassment, and anger. When he was finished, I asked the class to tell him how they felt when he had an accident and refused to change his clothes. They told him how they hated the smell and thought that he just wanted to be mean to them. He explained that he thought they would know and tease him more if he did change his clothes.

After communication was open between Steve and the class, I had Steve return to his desk. Steve was now a part of the group, and as such was expected to be part of the group problem-solving process. Steve agreed to change his clothes promptly if an accident occurred. The class agreed to stop all teasing and avoidance behaviors. Some of the students even apologized and hugged him spontaneously at the end of the discussion.

The changes in Steve and the group were immediate and dramatic after that experience. With most group problem-solving sessions, however, change takes place much more gradually. The groundwork for this kind of progress must be laid with effective limit setting during Stage One and active instruction of prerequisite skills during Stage Two. As students learn to identify emotions, manage behaviors, communicate effectively, and problem solve productively, they establish successful procedures to follow in a group setting. As those procedures become more automatic, Stage Three functioning begins.

STAGE THREE: INTERNALIZING LIMITS AND PROCEDURES

Stage Three is a period of relative calm and stability for the group. Driekurs and colleagues' (1982) four motivations for misbehavior have been addressed in Stage One and Stage Two. A need for power has been satisfied through clearly and consistently offered choices; opportunities to communicate and take responsibility for group decision making and problem solving; and individual as well as group goal attainment experiences. A need for revenge has been eliminated through effective self-assertion. Attention from peers and adults can be obtained most readily through appropriate behaviors taught, practiced, and reinforced within the group. Helplessness is no more useful than aggression in an atmosphere that honors the individual's power of choice. So, what is left for the teacher and students to do during Stage Three?

Stage Three is a period that is often overlooked or rushed in a push for inclusion. The lessons learned during Stage Two need time to become internalized and generalized to other settings and groups of people. Students need opportunities to experience difficulties and attempt to resolve them without immediate adult intervention, under the watchful eye of a teacher trained to intervene if that becomes necessary. Students need time to ease into new situations with new adults and classmates while still having time each day to return to the environment that nurtured their growth. Students need to practice these newly learned competencies in different settings while their EBD teacher moves farther and farther away.

In an effort to maximize positive outcomes and minimize problems, teachers often supervise too closely. Peers in regular education classrooms tease and get teased; have arguments and resolve them; and get frustrated with assignments and find a way to get through it on their own. During Stage Three, teachers need to increase opportunities for students to transfer skills to new settings while gradually decreasing their availability. If the teacher continues to manage the group during Stage Three with the same hovering attention of Stage One or direction of Stage Two, problems are likely to resurface and recycle. Regression will occur if opportunities for growth are inhibited.

An example of this phenomenon occurred with Trina and Jo. The two girls had hated each other during Stage One. The only time they formed an alliance was to defend themselves against the boys. During Stage Two, an understanding and friendship developed between them. As the group moved toward transitioning into new class experiences during Stage Three, the old animosity resurfaced. I quickly intervened each time. They would resolve that immediate issue quickly enough with my help but would be at each other's throats again before long. I decided, with much anxiety, to let them work out their differences without my help. As their next argument began, I asked them to step into the hall. I explained that I felt that they were ready to solve their own disputes. I promised to be nearby if they wanted or needed my assistance. They looked at me in amazement, watched me move down the hall, and then began arguing again. The volume reached an impressive level. They did not threaten physical assault, curse, or call each other names, so I waited in pained silence. Eventually, their voices returned to calm and quiet tones. I moved closer to them and asked if they were done. They nodded that they were. I congratulated them on their maturity in handling a difficult situation and reminded them of how differently that conversation would have ended at the beginning of the year. They laughed. The squabbles that had been so frequent ended. It was clearly time for me to get out of their way.

Many students have difficulty leaving the safety and security of an EBD classroom when mainstreaming begins. Giving students who are ready ample opportunities to use their newfound skills before leaving the sheltered environment of the special education classroom strengthens the internalization and generalization process necessary for future success.

TECHNIQUES FOR ALL THREE STAGES

Redl's and Wineman's (1965) Surface Behavior Management techniques are important at every stage of the group's development. Because rule reminders can inadvertently reinforce the inappropriate behavior, according to Irving and Martin (1982), the following techniques can be especially effective with students exhibiting EBD:

1. *Planned ignoring.* Behaviors that are exhibited for the purpose of seeking attention and do not spread or interfere with safety or group functioning are most effectively extinguished through planned ignoring. This technique should never be used with aggressive behaviors. The class may need to be taught to do this as well. Peer attention can be even more powerful than adult attention for some students.

2. *Signal interference.* If a student is calm enough to respond, has a positive relationship with the teacher, and is free from uncontrollable pathological impulses, a nonverbal signal may be all that is necessary to assist him or her in regaining focus. Guetzloe (n.d.a.) advocates teaching students to recognize a few of the universal sign language signals.

3. *Proximity and touch control.* Moving closer to a student in distress or placing a hand on the shoulder can be effective in showing support in a nonthreatening way. When using this technique, refrain from pointing out inappropriate behavior. Comment positively on any move toward compliance.

4. *Interest boosting.* Change the tempo or activity, comment on the student's work, or inquire about a known interest related to the assignment if a student shows signs of restlessness. Do this before off-task behavior occurs.

5. *Hypodermic affection.* Express genuine affection for or appreciation of a student to assist the student in regaining self-control.

6. *Easing tension through humor.* Humor can often stop undesirable behavior if it is used in a timely and positive manner. Sarcasm, cynicism, and aggression are not appropriate uses of humor. One example from the middle school group illustrated throughout this book fits nicely here.

The group's favorite epithet during Stage One was "Fuck this shit!" No amount of behavior modification or discussion of alternative phrases seemed to have an impact on this response. Finally, as Mark stood over me screaming "Fuck this shit!" in response to a consequence earned for another behavior, I looked up at him with a deadpan expression and asked, "Wouldn't that be kind of messy?" I am 5' 6 1/2" tall. Mark is 6' tall. If he had sensed any animosity or sarcasm from me, he probably would have knocked me to the floor. Instead, he slid his back down the wall, landed on the floor, and rolled with laughter. What had been a tense and threatening situation a few moments before became a warm and accepting opportunity for Mark and the whole group in terms of their relationship with me. Not only did Mark take responsibility for the behavior and consequence that sparked his repetition of the worn out phrase; but no one in the group ever repeated it again. When they heard students in other classes say it, they laughed. It became a private joke between me and the class.

7. *Hurdle help.* Before a student begins to act out, assist the student with a difficult section of an assignment or task.

8. *Regrouping.* Change the seating arrangement or the small-group assignments of students to avoid specific problems. Do this in a nonpunitive and, if possible, undetectable way.

9. *Restructuring.* If an activity is not successful, change it as quickly as possible. It is important to always have a back-up plan. Sometimes it is best to move from an interactive game to something like Bingo that requires no interaction. This can be done smoothly and nonpunitively when a group is becoming overstimulated. At other times, offering a choice might be more effective. Students could choose to cover information orally through discussion or copy notes from an overhead, for example.

10. *Direct appeal.* If a student or group has a positive relationship with the teacher, it is sometimes effective to just ask that a behavior stop due to the problems that it is creating. No consequence or reward is intended or implied. This is a simple, straightforward request from one person to another.

11. *Antiseptic bouncing.* Remove a student from a distressing situation before inappropriate behaviors occur. Be careful not to inadvertently reward a student who is instigating a problem.

12. *Support from routine.* Schedules and routines are often overlooked by adults when considering behavior management interventions. Knowing what to do and when to do it provides structure, security, and predictability in the lives of students who may not experience such support in other areas of their lives.

13. *Limiting space and tools.* Rather than taking away items that distract or create potential harm after a student is engaged with them, keep them out of sight and reach from the beginning. This is especially important during Stage One, when tantrums might escalate to unnecessarily dangerous or reinforcing proportions if too many items are available for throwing and breaking.

Although academic instruction cannot truly begin on higher levels of cognitive functioning until the group experiences satisfactory levels of safety, security, and trust, the academic and affective instruction can be managed in a way that enhances group development. Chapter 6 examines components of academic and affective instruction, strategies compatible with each group's stage of development, and curriculum considerations relative to a group's success.

6

Affective and Academic Instruction

"Oh, Merlyn," he cried, "please come too."

"For this once," . . . "But in future you will have to go by yourself. Education is experience, and the essence of experience is self-reliance."
—T. H. White

Teaching students to become self-reliant is the ultimate goal of instruction. When working with students in EBD classes, affective and academic instruction must be combined. There is not enough time in the day or money in most school budgets for segregating affective and academic issues. Teachers are more often than not called upon to teach social skills, self-help life skills, interpersonal problem-solving and communication skills, and academic content. This can appear overwhelming. With the assistance of a theoretical framework from which to base instructional decisions, however, a pattern of student needs clearly emerges. Maslow's hierarchy of human needs provides a basis for a progression from strict behavior modification to teacher-facilitated group decision making to cooperative discipline techniques in the maintenance of behavior management from Stage One to Stage Three. Krathwohl, Bloom, and Masia (1956) have provided further theoretical structuring for instructional decisions. A movement from mere awareness of social norms and recall of knowledge-level information to higher levels of social and cognitive functioning will occur only in a supportive, nurturing atmosphere. Table 6.1 illustrates the expected progression of growth.

STAGE ONE

At the lowest level of social-emotional functioning, children are just becoming aware that rules for behavior exist. Children at this level of functioning, according to Krathwohl and colleagues (1956), do not necessarily follow the rules or understand them, but they can state them. The next level of functioning on Krathwohl's hierarchy is marked by following rules relative to the rewards or punishments contingent upon the exhibited behaviors. Even though students in classes for EBD may be far beyond the chronological age expected for such low-level functioning, the group typically responds during Stage One at the two lowest levels identified on Table 6.1.

TABLE 6.1
Cognitive and Affective Levels

Affective Stages (Krathwohl et al., 1956)	Emotional Needs (Maslow, 1962)	Cognitive Stages (Bloom et al., 1956)
Stage One		
Level I		
Receiving: Aware of	Physiological	Knowledge: To know about
Level II		
Responding: Acts out of external expectations	Safety and Security	Comprehension: To understand
Stage Two		
Level III		
Valuing: Preference	Belonging, Love, and Social Activity	Application: Put to use
Stage Three		
Level IV		
Organization: Establish a value system	Self-respect and Respect of Others	Analysis: Break into parts
		Synthesis: Create
Level V		
*Characterization: To live by one's beliefs	*Self-Actualization	Evaluation: To judge for a purpose

*These levels generally are not reached before adulthood.

Because emotionality effects cognitive functioning, the Taxonomy of Cognitive Development (Bloom, Englehart, Frost, Hill, & Krathwohl, 1956) illustrates the relationship between group functioning in social-emotional areas and instructional needs. A group that requires external control to maintain order and safety will need academic material that can be mastered with a minimum of frustration. For this reason, Bloom's lowest level of cognitive functioning is the focus for academic instruction. This level is defined as the Knowledge level. Information is retained with the ability to recall. Higher levels of processing information are not required at this point. The internal control necessary for the management of risk taking and the tolerance for frustration inherent in higher-level cognitive tasks have not been established. Stage One is an excellent time to build a sense of mastery by reinforcing students for concrete evidence of achievement. Teachers can take time during Stage One to teach basic skills in preparation for the Application, Analysis, and Synthesis activities that will be introduced later.

Stage One affective instruction is most supportive when students are taught factual-, knowledge-, and comprehension-level information. Stage One affective instruction would include identification and expansion of vocabulary necessary for communicating emotions and needs, relaxation instruction, self-acceptance, and social skills instruction.

There are many books, videos, and software packages on the market that address the affective instructional needs outlined above. Selection of curriculum materials in this area would depend on the age and functioning level of the group. A list of resource materials is found in the Appendix. After a discussion of precision teaching (PT) and direct instruction (DI), teacher-developed activities that are supportive of Stage One academic and affective needs will be examined.

Precision Teaching

Precision teaching (PT) is a behaviorally based instructional strategy. Bender (1992) defined PT as follows:

> Precision teaching—an instructional monitoring approach developed by Lindsley that is based on daily curriculum-based assessment procedures, and features use of a standard measurement chart and frequent measures of learning rate. (Bender, 1992, p. 391)

Components of PT are described by Sulzer-Azaroff and Mayer (1986) as follows:

1. Skills and concepts are carefully defined and sequentially ordered.

2. Performance is measured frequently.

3. Feedback is immediate and corrective.

4. Instruction is designed to maximize the opportunities for correct responses and positive feedback.

5. Recording of successive performance rates is provided.

6. Stimulus control is used to increase correct response rates.

7. Maintenance and retention procedures are planned and programmed into the instructional strategy rather than being left to chance.

8. Small-group as well as individual instruction is possible.

PT does not dictate instructional methodology, require the teacher to follow a previously prepared script, or rely on any one particular set of instructional materials, according to Bender (1992). For that reason, PT can be widely adapted across age groups and content areas.

Research by Gleason (1991) supports the use of PT as a strategy for teaching knowledge-level information. In the 1991 study, students who were taught information in small, cumulative segments learned the material three times faster than students who were presented with a large volume of material initially. PT provides the positive reinforcement, concrete measure of progress, and clearly defined tasks that are so essential to the support of Stage One needs.

Direct Instruction

Direct instruction (DI) was defined by Bender (1992) as

a teacher-led, instructional procedure in that students are provided with specific instructions on the task, modeling, teacher-led practice, independent practice, and frequent feedback on their performance. (Bender, 1992, p. 385)

DI is like PT in that both establish clearly defined parameters for lesson completion and mastery as well as providing a success-oriented procedure with ample practice and evaluation. DI differs from PT in the use of a more controlled and repetitive delivery of instruction. Many materials specifically marketed as being based on DI provide teachers with strict guidelines for lesson presentation, the introduction of successive skills, and the use of support materials or lesson variations. Some DI packages even include a script for the teacher to follow.

Comparison of PT and DI

While PT techniques can be used across content areas with greater flexibility in the areas of presentation and practice of information, DI does provide a predictable, success-oriented structure that many students find reassuring initially. The primary goal of Stage One is the establishment of safety, order, and structure. Students who find themselves in a predictable environment where appropriate behavior is rewarded, inappropriate behavior is prohibited, physical and social-emotional needs are respected, and learning is actively engaging and success oriented will reach a satisfactory level of stability.

Classroom Activities

The teacher can facilitate this movement by providing the following activities and procedures:

1. *Demystify any process students are expected to learn or follow.* Whereas students who have experienced a great deal of success in the past might welcome a challenge, students in special classes often feel threatened by new material. Integrating unfamiliar concepts into content areas that have already been mastered provides a level of comfort that allows learning to proceed more smoothly. For example, many students find the concept of equivalent fractions to be difficult. These students know their colors. For the first few days, blocks or strips of construction paper can be used to represent halves, fourths, thirds, sixths, eighths, and one whole. Each fractional part can be represented by a different color. Students can be asked to find out how many pinks equal a green, or how many blues equal a yellow. Slowly, the fraction names, written symbols, and computation strategies can be incorporated into the lessons. Students can be reminded that this is something they have already mastered at one level. It helps them to know that they understand the concept and are just learning new words to describe it.

2. *Break learning tasks into manageable parts without appearing condescending.* Most students are capable at a cognitive level of completing a science project or some other complex task, but they lack the past experiences with planning, self-confidence, impulse control, and organizational skills that are necessary for success. These skills and competencies can be taught through modeling and careful teacher planning. The teacher can do a task analysis of the proposed learning activity. The first time students are assigned such a task, the teacher will take them through the steps one at a time as a whole group. For example, if students are to complete a

science project, the teacher will help them select an appropriate topic one day, write an appropriate research question with identified control and experimental variables the next day, make a list of materials to use and procedures to follow the following day, and so on. After going through the process a few times as a whole group, partners or individuals can begin to complete project planning sheets on their own with the teacher acting as a facilitator or consultant to the project.

Never assume that students can do complex, multistep assignments alone. Even very academically talented students may experience high levels of anxiety if presented with an unfamiliar task that appears too overwhelming.

3. *Move from concrete, to pictorial, to abstract in the presentation of any new concept.* Math instruction often follows this progression. It is equally effective in all areas of instruction. Science, social studies, and language arts lessons involve understanding many vocabulary words that may not be part of the students' prior experiences. The use of all possible modalities increases the likelihood that students will comprehend and retain the information presented.

4. *Begin a class photograph album.* Start with a page dedicated to each student. Have each student write a brief autobiography. Include the typed or computer printed information with the photograph of each student. Include pictures and information about the teacher and any other adult who works closely with the class. Add group pictures and descriptions of activities as the year progresses. The written material can be obtained through a teacher-directed group writing lesson during Stage One. As the class gains more self-control, partners can be assigned to complete sections for the album.

The advantages of this ongoing group project are both cognitive and affective. It gives meaning and structure to written language lessons. The computer or typewriter becomes a valuable tool of instruction as spelling, capitalization, and punctuation skills are highlighted. The class has a written record of the positive events the students have experienced together. The album promotes a sense of belonging to the group while simultaneously honoring each individual. For students who enter later in the year, the album becomes a way to share the group's past while welcoming the newcomers in the present. Finally, the album provides a way for the group to share with other staff and students in the school. It can be put on display in the office or media center from time to time. Positive feedback given verbally or in the form of written notes builds motivation and group affiliation.

5. *Make class anthologies of poems, stories, reports, and illustrations.* The initial class-produced books may be a collection of items generated through teacher-directed whole group writing lessons, a compilation of individually completed assignments, or a combination of the two. Students benefit from the process academically by being involved in the following activities:

a. *Prewriting strategies.* Before beginning the actual writing activity, students will need to be encouraged to list vocabulary and ideas to be included in the manuscript. These thoughts may need to be focused, expanded, or put in some kind of sequential order. Whole group instruction and teacher modeling are essential initially. Many students perceive writing to be so far removed from their abilities and experiences that they avoid the process out of a sense of inadequacy. Pantomime and oral presentations related to the writing assignment can help some students bridge the gap in their personal experiences between nonverbal, verbal, and written forms of communication.

b. *Teacher-directed whole group writing.* This strategy is taken from the proponents of language experience. After discussing a topic common to all members of the class, the teacher acts as a scribe and facilitator in the production of a group-dictated story, report, or poem. Every group member is encouraged to contribute to the product by suggesting content, organization of concepts, and editorial changes. The advantages to beginning with teacher-directed whole group writing activities are that the writing process is modeled for students in a nonthreatening way, group ownership in the finished product is strengthened, and skill instruction can be managed on many levels simultaneously without singling out individual weaknesses or wasting valuable instructional time. The first draft of the whole group product should be kept on large chart paper or an overhead transparency. This allows the teacher and group to proofread and edit before a final draft is handwritten or typed. Each student can write or type his or her own copy for inclusion in a portfolio or bound anthology later.

c. *Producing the final product.* Once the class has accumulated the desired number of items for the completion of a book, everyone can be involved in the process of organizing, devising a table of contents and dedication page, collating, and binding the books. Binding machines can be used if they are available. Students can make cardboard and plastic self-adhesive book covers if other types of binding are not available. Instructions for this type of book construction are found in the Appendix.

Affective advantages to the production of a class book include the sense of accomplishment and mastery such activities provide, the positive attention students receive from others for the effort such products represent, a strengthening of appropriate identity with a group achievement, and a belief in personal abilities to succeed academically.

6. *Make a bulletin board or display that requires students to combine their individual efforts to form a completed whole.* This is most effective when the project is related to both an affective and an academic theme. A more complete description of the development and use of themes is found at the end of this chapter. An example of a possible project would include the construction of an early English settlement from pretzels, milk cartons, twigs, and various other items. The academic focus may center on colonization and the beginnings of democracy in the United States. The affective focus might revolve around the need for rules, laws, authority, cooperation, and active participation in decision making. As individuals build log cabins for inclusion in the town, the focus begins to shift from "I did this" to "We made this." The class can name the town, decide on rules or laws for the town, label streets, make a map, write a book, and use the display as an academic and affective tool for learning and motivation.

7. *Play games initially that require individual participation without interaction.* Students who have not learned to trust the teacher, each other, and themselves are not ready for unstructured, overstimulating activities. Building the belief that the class can have fun together takes care and planning. Bingo is an excellent example of a Stage One game. Other games can be devised from the academic material being taught. Rapidly paced question-and-answer type games that reinforce factual academic content can be adjusted so all students are included at their individual academic levels simultaneously. For example, spelling words, math facts, or reading vocabulary might be placed on color-coded cards for students. Each student is asked questions based on the cards from his or her stack. Scores can be kept on the chalkboard. One point can be awarded for attempting

and another for a correct answer. No one loses! Everyone earns a small reward for each point earned. Some students will inevitably earn more points than others. Make sure everyone wins something, however, even if it is just for participation. Jeopardy, Wheel of Fortune, and Concentration are game formats that are easily adaptable to academic content.

8. *Cook.* Food is a universal reinforcer. Plan a weekly cooking activity. Foods are easily incorporated into academic lessons on nutrition, plants, social studies topics, sequencing, and following written or oral directions. Start with recipes that individuals can prepare in isolation. Move to items that require each student to complete a part of the recipe for everyone in the group. When the class is ready, introduce cooperative recipes with more complex procedures. The more complex activities should be saved for Stage Two and Stage Three. Good Stage One recipes include the following:

   a. *Pudding.* Give each student a cup, a plastic spoon, 2 tablespoons of dry instant pudding mix, and 1/2 cup of milk. Each student stirs the mixture until the pudding thickens. The teacher might like to provide a whipped topping as well.

   b. *Fruit or vegetable salad.* Give each student a plastic knife, a paper plate, and a piece of fruit or a vegetable to slice. The teacher brings a large bowl to each student's desk, assembles the ingredients, adds dressing if desired, and serves the salad.

   c. *Paint on bread.* Put 1 or 2 tablespoons of milk in several small containers. Add food coloring. Use clean paintbrushes to paint designs on the bread. Toast the bread. The colors will appear bright against the toasted edges of the bread. Add honey if desired.

   d. *Bread pudding.* Have seven students each tear one slice of bread into small pieces. Put 2 cups of milk and 1 tablespoon of margarine in a microwave on high for 3 minutes. Stir 1 beaten egg, 1 teaspoon of cinnamon, and 1 teaspoon of vanilla into the milk mixture. Add the bread and 1/2 cup of raisins. Place in a microwave on high for 9 minutes. Cool and serve.

   e. *Cheese wagons.* Make or purchase pimento cheese spread. Wash and slice celery into 2- to 3-inch sections. Wash and slice carrots into thin, round, wheel-shaped slices. Use toothpicks to attach the carrot wheels to the sides of the celery. Fill the wagons with the cheese spread. Peanut butter can be used instead of cheese if desired.

   f. *Critters.* Purchase large and miniature marshmallows and toothpicks. Challenge students to make insects or other animals out of them.

Many favorite recipes can be adapted for school use. A list of cookbooks written especially for classroom use is provided in the Appendix. Before beginning any cooking program, teach prerequisite safety rules. Refrain from using recipes that require the use of a hot plate, sharp knives, or other potentially hazardous materials until the class is well under control.

Theme Development

In addition to using of the strategies and activities discussed previously, developing a thematic approach can enhance academic and affective instruction even further. Hobbs (1982) described group development in relation to studies and projects. Rhodes (1965) suggested integrated units of study for students in classrooms for EBD. Themes have many advantages, including the following:

1. They provide an instructional focus for students who may be easily distracted.

2. They provide a concrete link between subject areas for students who may not make such connections easily on their own.

3. They can increase interest and motivation by making academic content more relevant to students.

4. They provide a framework that will support varying academic functioning levels simultaneously.

5. They provide academic and affective instruction in an integrated format that strengthens and reinforces both areas.

6. They enhance student mastery by immersing students in the concepts, vocabulary, and scope of a topic.

In planning for a thematic unit, the teacher should:

1. Identify student needs and interests.

2. Identify information that can be acquired at the recall level relative to students' needs and possible themes.

3. Identify process skills students need that could be incorporated into possible themes. Process skills include all higher-level comprehension, application, analysis, synthesis, and evaluation skills necessary in problem solving.

4. Examine the existing curriculum for possible theme ideas and instructional materials.

5. Arrange any existing units around the theme or themes selected.

6. Collect supporting materials from community resources, the school media center, or through retail purchases.

7. When beginning instruction, start with previously learned concepts.

8. Build the students' knowledge base carefully to avoid frustration and to enhance self-esteem.

9. Introduce process skills with concrete objects. Move to the use of diagrams or pictures. When students have achieved mastery of a concept, proceed with abstract examples. To illustrate this process, imagine presenting students with the problem of needing to buy a certain number of objects with a limited amount of money. In the initial lessons, students could be encouraged to manipulate empty cans, boxes, and other items to be purchased while having access to play money and price tags for each item. At a later date, pictures from a newspaper or magazine could be substituted for the real items. Play money and price tags might still be needed. Finally, a list of items with the accompanying prices and a spending limit might be all students need in order to complete the task. Starting with the abstract task could overwhelm students. The use of real items followed by pictures and, finally, word and price lists alone, allows students to build a repertoire of skills with a minimum of resistance.

10. Start with a few variables. Increase the number of variables as students demonstrate mastery. As in the example given in item 9, initial problems may require students to budget two or three items. As their ability to manage money and manipulate information increases, other concepts can be added. Students may be asked to budget more items, incorporate the use of coupons within the monetary allotment, or compare items of differing sizes and prices to determine the most cost-effective purchases. These additional variables should only be added as students gain mastery over preliminary information and process skills.

11. Provide practice with process skills in as many different subject areas as possible. For example, a Venn diagram can be used to help students compare and contrast information in math, science, social studies, language arts, and reading. As students make use of process skills across subject areas, they begin to learn how to learn. Higher level thinking strategies become integrated into an overall approach to understanding, organizing, problem solving, and using information effectively. This is the cognitive equivalent to behavioral maintenance and generalization.

12. Be prepared to shift to recall-level activities during times of increased stress. When a substitute teacher has to be called, a new student enters, interruptions occur in the schedule, or students are experiencing unusual amounts of anxiety, have activities ready that reinforce knowledge acquisition. Fill-in-the-blank worksheets with a word bank, word searches with clues for key vocabulary, computation drills, question-and-answer games such as Jeopardy, and matching-type worksheets or games can be useful. Students under high levels of stress do not have the energy necessary to tackle demanding cognitive tasks. Return to higher-level activities when students are calm.

13. Keep theme topics broad enough to sustain interest and a variety of activities over an extended period of time. Students in classes for EBD often miss time in class due to behavior problems, illnesses, or absences. If a theme only lasts 10 school days and a student misses 3 days during that 10-day period, 30% of the information will not have been available for learning. If a theme is planned to last 20 school days, the teacher has more flexibility in planning strategies that will increase all students' knowledge and process skills while providing the instruction missed by the student who has been absent. Themes that are extended over a longer period of time have more potential for encouraging school and class attendance. Students begin to look forward to the development of theme information and activities. They feel successful. As more time is spent on academic achievement, less time is taken for acting out or avoiding school.

One very effective Stage One theme is sports. It appeals to a wide range of ages, can be applied to varying academic functioning levels, and supports affective as well as academic needs. Biographies of sports figures, newspaper articles, statistics, health, physical science, graphs, charts, and qualities of successful athletes and teams are just a few of the areas that can be studied. A behavior management bulletin board can create a positive and face-saving environment to establish order and safety. It is not considered "wimpy" to listen to the coach, support a team in a positive way, or practice an athletic skill until it is mastered. Relating such lessons to the classroom can motivate and stimulate growth. A sample unit plan for sports can be found in the Appendix.

If PT, DI, and themes work so well during Stage One, why do anything else? Stage One is the foundation. Rules have not become internalized. Academic content has not been stretched to include all the higher-level thinking and process skills students will need in order to function successfully in the world beyond the class for EBD. Once the foundation of control has been established, it is important to shift to Stage Two instructional and affective strategies.

STAGE TWO

The next level on Krathwohl's hierarchy, as shown in Table 6.1, is *valuing*. At this level, students are beginning to decide which rules are of value to them. Questions about the reasons for certain rules arise. Rather than respond as if threatened, it is best to answer questions in a matter-of-fact fashion, refuse to argue, and accept the student's right to disagree in theory as long as behaviors remain appropriate.

Cognitive functioning, according to Bloom and colleagues (1956), moves from knowledge to comprehension to application. By Stage Two, students have enough self-control to begin to apply some of the information learned during Stage One to problem-solving situations. Students can now begin peer tutoring in highly structured settings, group problem solving, and group decision making. The affective lessons continue to stress relaxation instruction and social skills acquisition, with a new emphasis on interpersonal communication skills.

Effective Stage Two affective development includes the following four elements:

1. Teaching students to be aware of nonverbal communication cues in themselves and others.

2. The importance of using what Canfield (1986) referred to as "I" messages when expressing emotions.

3. Cognitive behavioral strategies.

4. Actively providing opportunities for what Seligman (1991) called "learned optimism."

Students are often unaware of how their nonverbal communication contributes to the escalation of problems between them and others. Proximity, facial expressions, tone and volume of voice, posture, and gestures carry powerful messages to others. Especially in schools with marked cultural differences among staff and students, these issues will require a great deal of time and attention. Videos, role plays, observations of others, examination of photographs, and class discussions can be used to increase student awareness of the importance of respecting another's comfort. Target behaviors for use with the class behavior management plan can also be identified for students. Individual or group goals can be established to help students refine their own behaviors or their responses to others' behaviors in this area.

Canfield (1986), in *Self-Esteem in the Classroom*, included a section on the use of "I" messages. Students learn to express their feelings without attacking the self-worth of others. As this skill is taught and practiced during affective instruction, it can be incorporated into the classroom hierarchy of consequences. Students who are able to remember to use "I" messages from the beginning of an encounter can be awarded bonus points or other privileges. Students who are willing to rephrase an inappropriate attack on another with an appropriate "I" message can receive a less severe consequence than the student who is unwilling to apply this newly learned skill.

Rational-emotive strategies originated with Ellis (1980) and are an essential component of affective learning at this point in the group's development. Rational-emotive strategies are effective in cognitive behavioral training for the following reasons:

1. Students learn to separate their emotional responses to events from their behavioral responses. In the beginning, they tend to believe that they have no choice. They believe that if someone makes them mad they must hit. Anger and hitting are understood to be synonymous. Rational behavioral strategies help them understand that although emotions, physiological reactions, thoughts, and behaviors are closely related, they are not one and the same.

2. Students learn that physiological responses to fear or anger are healthy and normal. The tension they experience is experienced by everyone to some degree or another in stressful situations.

3. Students learn that the degree of stress they experience is related to the things they believe about a situation. If they change their beliefs, they modify the intensity of the emotion.

4. Students learn that even when emotions are extremely intense, behaviors are derived from choices. The choices made are reflective of the beliefs.

5. Because the things students tell themselves can be changed, behavior choices can be changed.

A word of caution using cognitive behavioral materials: Students must be led into these understandings through a series of lessons and experiences. This information cannot be imposed upon an unwilling, captive audience. It took me about 3 weeks to bring a class of middle school students to the understanding that emotions and behaviors are not synonymous. Many times over the course of those lessons, I had to restrain my impulse to preach. The lessons, questions, and experiences eventually led the group to accept and take ownership of this concept. The day it happened, I watched in amazement as smiles, laughter, and a "She got us!" from the peer leader spread around the room. A commitment to learn more and to change grew out of that experience that no amount of preaching or breast beating could have accomplished.

Cognitive behavioral materials appropriate for different ages of students are listed in the Appendix.

The fourth component of effective Stage Two affective instruction is often orchestrated by the teacher. The elements of Seligman's (1991) concept of "learned optimism" should be present throughout all three stages of group development. During Stage Two, however, the group can begin to discuss openly the different ways academic and behavioral success occur in the classroom setting. The idea that their choices determine the resulting consequences to a large degree builds a sense of mastery, self-esteem, the ability to generalize skills and information from one setting to the next, and a belief that the students have some degree of control over their lives in positive, meaningful ways. Teachers can encourage the acquisition of a sense of learned optimism by employing the following strategies:

1. Provide instructional activities that build upon prior knowledge.

2. Pace instruction for success.

3. Reward achievement consistently. Keep records for future reference. Stress the relationship between effort and results.

4. Make consequences for inappropriate behavior instructional and logical, to stress the link between behavioral choices and the resulting consequences.

5. Use the rational behavioral strategies learned during affective lessons to reinforce feelings of empowerment.

6. Make the classroom environment as predictable and positive as possible at all times. Reinforce the expectation that the future is bright and worthy of hope as well as personal effort. Academic as well as affective lessons and interactions can reflect this belief. Students can learn to approach each day with a sense of optimism when they feel safe, valued, and in control of what happens to them.

Seligman (1991), Kerr (1987), and Vernon (1989 a, b) subscribe to the following five-step approach in teaching rational behavioral strategies and optimism to students:

1. Identify beliefs.

2. Dispute irrational beliefs.

3. Substitute rational thoughts.

4. Act on the new thoughts.

5. Evaluate the consequences.

Kerr's (1987) book *Positively! Learning to Manage Negative Emotions* takes students through a sequential set of lessons designed to help them identify the components of this equation: $B + H = C$ and $C = F/D$. Translated, the equation means that Beliefs plus Happenings equal Consequences; and Consequences equal Feelings as well as what is Done.

The strategies suggested with cognitive behavioral techniques and Seligman's learned optimism relate well to Braxton's (1993) recommendation that students be taught appropriate self-assertion skills and to Heuchart's and Long's (1981) description of the use of life space interviewing (LSI) with individuals and groups. LSI was first developed by Redl and Wineman (1965). Its five long-range goals include:

1. Helping students perceive an event accurately.

2. Helping students understand the full impact of a behavior.

3. Helping students discover or develop a value system that can effectively control destructive impulses.

4. Helping students develop a repertoire of social skills from which to select the most appropriate behavior for a given situation.

5. Helping students develop healthy self-preserving boundaries.

Before beginning LSI with an individual or group of students, the teacher will need to examine the following components of a situation:

1. Is the issue pertinent to success within the group?

2. Is the student sufficiently aware of the issue? A student who is unaware of an issue or rigidly denies the existence of a problem may not be ready to deal with a discussion in a productive manner. Respect the developmental process. Do not attempt to force a student or a group into a discussion before prerequisite skills and awareness levels are established.

3. Be aware of the relationship as well as the role inherent in the teacher–student exchange. According to Redl and Wattenburg (1951, as cited in Charles, 1992), teachers represent to students combinations of the following roles:

- Representatives of society.
- Judges.
- Sources of knowledge.
- Helpers in learning
- Referees.
- Detectives.
- Models.

- Caretakers.
- Ego supporters.
- Group leaders.
- Surrogate parents.
- Targets for hostility.
- Friends and confidantes.
- Objects of affection.

Compatibility of the teacher's role and relationship with a student or group with the content of the LSI is crucial to the success of this strategy.

4. The LSI is a potentially conflict-ridden exchange. It is advisable to be aware of stress levels in the teacher as well as the students. It is important to assess mood manageability before beginning the LSI. The LSI will not be effective if it results in a loss of control by the teacher, student, or group.

5. Timing is crucial. All parties, including the teacher, must be calm enough to begin. Waiting too long after an event to begin processing, however, weakens the effect of the LSI. In addition to the interval between a problem and the verbal processing about the problem, scheduling of other events must be considered. A student who expects to go to lunch in 3 minutes will not have his mind on the issue being addressed in the LSI.

6. The environment in which a problem occurred is the best one in which to conduct the LSI. This is not always possible. When it is, the verbal processing can be tested by the reality of site-specific information and content.

The LSI model comprises a seven-step process as outlined by Fagen (1981):

Step 1. Provide emotional first aid by allowing the student to express feelings without making judgments about them. If this is done in a group setting, make sure that each student gets an opportunity to speak. No name calling or blaming will be tolerated. Acceptance of feelings will be unconditional.

Step 2. Establish a definition of the problem. What events took place? Who was involved? Where did the problem occur?

Step 3. Clarify the events, how they were sequenced, and the issues involved.

Step 4. Examine the problem in terms of how prevalent it is. Does this problem occur often, with many different people, across settings? Is this an isolated event for this student? The depth and spread of the problem are important considerations in determining solutions. For this reason, the teacher needs to be aware of this component in the problem-solving process.

Step 5. Before proceeding to problem-solving issues, reestablish the initial communication of acceptance. Students may not be able to identify their emotions. Reflecting on the emotional content of the problem conveys a regard for the student as an individual and simultaneously instructs. Statements such as "I see how angry you are. Your fists are clenched"; "I know this is hard for you to discuss. Your head is down" help students feel understood and regain self-control. It is important to refrain from making value judgments at this time.

Step 6. Ask questions that will elicit student-generated solution ideas. Guide the student or group through a list of alternative behaviors. Develop a specific plan based on student-suggested ideas. The teacher helps to guide and direct this phase. The teacher's authority is not undermined or given to the student or group. The teacher's authority becomes a framework and support for the emerging self-control of each individual and the group as a whole.

A typical Stage Two problem began to plague the middle school class introduced earlier. The frequent challenges of authority, fighting, and explosive problems experienced during Stage One had stopped. Individuals had problems from time to time, but the group as a whole functioned fairly well. Encouraged by the growth I was seeing, I offered to help the class plan a field trip to a local park complete with a cook-out. The group could earn the trip by amassing a targeted number of collective star days. Each time I set criteria, the group proceeded to sabotage the trip with fighting, truancy, and noncompliance with everyday routines.

I held a group meeting. The group recognized the sabotaging behavior. I asked whether they really wanted the trip and the cook-out. They said that they did. I asked whether the criterion was fair. They said that it was. I asked for their help in understanding the problem. After some discussion, they revealed that they were worried about appearing to look like "nerds." Their definition of a nerd was someone who did everything a teacher asked, studied all the time, and did not know how to blend with peers. I accepted their fear of becoming nerds and tried to reassure them that they were in no danger.

Their solution to this problem was to take over the responsibility for earning the trip, monitoring the group's progress, and recordkeeping chores. They requested that I type the criterion for the trip and place it in a large manila envelope. This envelope would be placed on a counter in the room. Students interested in earning the trip would read the criterion and sign the sheet. A student-selected committee of three recorded grades, kept logs of completed work and behavior points, and updated the group graph of star days daily. My job was to teach and wait for them to tell me when to start the paperwork for a field trip request.

I did my job; they did theirs. We had a wonderful time at the cook-out. The process taught me the importance of including students in the search for solutions. During Stage One, they needed my benevolent dictatorship to establish control and limits not yet internalized. By Stage Two, they were ready to assume levels of responsibility that were directly taught and modeled for them. I believe that we invite regression when we do not allow for a gradual shift of control from external to internal means.

How does this shift manifest itself in the academic instructional areas? During Stage Two, students are ready to move beyond mere memorization and comprehension tasks as defined on Bloom's (1956) Taxonomy of Cognitive Development. The poor impulse control as exhibited through behaviors outlined on Selman's (1991) chart of assimilative and accommodative behaviors, has been sufficiently modified through behavior modification and the establishment of safety and security to allow students to begin more demanding cognitive and social-emotional tasks. A look at peer tutoring and the thematic, integrated approach to teaching provides valuable insights and strategies for instruction that supports the group's growth while encouraging movement to new levels of functioning.

Peer Tutoring

Peer tutoring, among its other advantages, is an excellent way to teach students the prerequisite social skills necessary for successful participation in cooperative learning activities. The teacher cannot assume that students know how to work together, even if the class has been relatively calm and controlled. To participate in activities that require active involvement with others to reach higher levels of application, analysis, synthesis, and evaluation in cognitive areas, students will need carefully controlled experiences with each other under less stressful academic situations while learning what to do and say during times of disagreement. Procedures for implementing and maintaining peer tutoring sessions in special education classrooms are delineated in an article by Kohler, Richardson, Mina, Dinwiddie, and Greenwood (1985). The following guidelines for initiating a peer tutoring program in the classroom were gleaned from this article:

1. Assigned each student to a dyad.

2. Teach each student to be a tutor as well as a tutee.

3. Assign specific duties to each role. Discuss and practice appropriate responses for students to use in each role during whole group instruction before dyads begin to work together.

4. When dyads do begin working together, keep the sessions brief.

5. Have tutors and tutees assist each other with highly structured content-level information such as spelling words correctly or identifying correct answers to targeted math facts. (Save more complex academic tasks such as proofreading written work or generating possible solutions to an application question for Stage Three, when students have had sufficient experience with the social skills required to be successful.)

6. Reward student dyads for appropriate social skills as well as academic achievement.

As students become skilled at both the tutor and tutee roles, sessions can be lengthened. The introduction of more than two students working together without direct adult supervision should be reserved for Stage Three group development.

Use thematic integrated units of study in conjunction with peer tutoring to support individual and group needs while encouraging further social-emotional and cognitive growth. The next section describes an effective Stage Two unit and the components necessary for group development.

Stage Two Theme: Plants

A thematic unit on plants provides a rich array of opportunities to build on the established structure of the group's functioning. Academic work can move smoothly from individual, knowledge-based achievement to partnerships in simple experiments, peer tutoring, and projects. Affective growth can be nurtured through an awareness of the positive interdependence of the group members. Family trees may not be productive projects to pursue due to personal problems individual students may encounter with that type of assignment. The development of an alternative representation of support is a valuable project. This may begin with a classroom bulletin board containing a tree. Each member of the class can be assigned a branch. Leaves can be added to each branch with specific items of information about each student. Each leaf could contain a different set of facts about each student. Categories of information could include likes, dislikes, accomplishments, goals, and contributions to the class. This bulletin board can be constructed over a period of weeks. Students could extend this idea to their personal lives. Even if their families are not available, they can identify the people with whom they have positive relationships. They can then make charts that help them identify their systems of support from a combination of school, community, and family resources.

Social skills can be gradually increased through more frequent and more demanding partnership assignments. As students are ready, the partnerships can move from simple peer tutoring exchanges to more involved cooperative problem-solving ventures. The important things for teachers to remember during Stage Two are as follows:

1. Individuals within the group are no more likely to be homogeneous in their social-emotional development than they are in their cognitive development.

2. Stage Two is a transitional stage between the need for a consistent, well-defined external structure of control and a more democratic, cooperative model of shared responsibility that requires higher levels of internalized control.

3. For the reasons stated above, the teacher must be ready at each moment to return in a nonpunitive way to higher levels of external control when individuals exhibit a need for such structure.

A plant theme allows for a great deal of flexibility with regard to these three points because most activities can be done alone or with a partner as students' needs dictate. A complete lesson plan for implementing a plant theme in the classroom is outlined in the Appendix. Activities that enhance individual and group growth begin with a plant "adoption" nursery. Prospective "parents" select seeds, plant them, learn about seed formation and germination, are awarded germination certificates when their seeds sprout, and begin to keep the equivalent of baby books on their plants. They record watering dates and amounts, keep a growth chart, write germination announcements, and make plans for relocating the seedling when it is ready to leave the nursery. Research skills are taught and used in the selection of a suitable environment for the plant. Beyond the classroom nursery experience, students can conduct various experiments; take field trips to local parks to identify native foliage; listen to guest speakers on various career opportunities in agriculture, forestry, conservation, landscaping, and horticulture; launch a study of nutrition based on fruits, vegetables, and grains; explore art forms based on found object sculptures and natural inks and dyes; or develop a school-based xeriscape study area. No matter what direction the theme takes, the benefits in terms of motivation, integration of subject matter, focused attention, and inclusiveness of all students' abilities will remain a strength of this approach.

STAGE THREE

Stage Three represents a period of generalization during which students commit themselves to rules, standards, and expectations that were previously taught, modeled, and reinforced by authority figures. Any age-appropriate theme, activity, or strategy can be used. During Stage Three greater emphasis should be placed on higher-level thinking skills and the transfer of appropriate social-emotional responses from one person or setting to a broad range of school and community experiences. Visits to other classrooms, guest speakers, and greater involvement in mainstreamed activities should be carefully planned, monitored, and increased in frequency as well as duration of time as students' behaviors indicate their readiness.

One effective Stage Three theme is economics. It provides students with adequate structure, a full range of academic experiences, and ample opportunities to explore problem-solving strategies in academic and interpersonal situations.

A full explanation of the economics unit used during Stage Three development is provided in the Appendix. A major strength of this unit for Stage Three groups is the incorporation of cooperative learning activities. The following section will explore the essential components of cooperative learning and the advantages of combining precision teaching (PT) with cooperative learning to enhance and accelerate academic, social, and emotional growth.

Planning, Documentation, and Consultation

*What we must decide is how we are valuable
rather than how valuable we are.*
—E.Z. Friedenburg

Planning, documentation, and consultation form the backbone of effective instruction and behavior management. With a group development model that simultaneously supports the immediate needs of a group and promotes growth to the next level, all components must be synchronized. Academic content must follow a scope and sequence that ensures success. Instructional strategies must be tailored to academic content as well as social-emotional abilities. Affective instruction must not be confined to one period a day. Opportunities to learn and practice social skills, problem-solving skills, communication skills, and self-management skills must permeate the program. To bring all components together into an effective, success-oriented approach, planning, documentation, and consultation must occur regularly. The next three sections will provide helpful guidelines in establishing and streamlining these vital areas of concern.

PLANNING

Effective planning occurs long before students arrive on the first day of school. Even before getting a class list, the teacher can begin planning. Knowing state and local requirements for instruction is helpful in organizing units of study around academic themes. The teacher can plan possible project, bulletin board, field trip, and enrichment activities around instructional units. Materials, guest speakers, and community resources can be located or at least listed. I find it helpful to make a file folder for each theme with community resources, films, guest speaker information, and addresses for support materials written on it. A theme planning chart like the one provided in the Appendix can be partially completed ahead of time with weekly subtitles, read-aloud literature titles, and resources that relate to the focus each particular week. Any worksheets, photographs, recipes, game ideas, newspaper clippings, or other resources related to the topic are placed in the folder. Throughout the year, I can easily add to the folder as items become available. A notebook or ledger with subject dividers is also useful for keeping theme resource information together.

After receiving a class list, the teacher can begin selecting specific academic skills by examining school records on each student. Testing can often be misleading. Students in classes for EBD often have gaps in their learning that interfere with accurate test results even when behavioral and emotional issues are taken into consideration. While final decisions on day-to-day instructional content must wait for direct contact with students, preliminary selection of materials can begin.

The teacher can begin to develop behavior management decisions around information in school records about placement behaviors. Initial classroom rules should target issues the group is likely to encounter. Keeping problems small and manageable by focusing on behaviors that lead to bigger problems such as name calling, play fighting, or leaving class without permission is an important first step. Using the Group Planning Sheet provided in the Appendix to analyze individual as well as group strengths and needs can make Stage One more successful for everyone. Stage One is by definition the most stormy. The teacher must do everything possible to reduce the intensity, frequency, and/or duration of stressful events during this stage. Later, as students move through Stage Two and Stage Three, planning for gradual changes in behavior management strategies and the introduction of different instructional strategies must continue. A shift from one stage to the next will become apparent through the examination of carefully documented changes within individuals and the group.

DOCUMENTATION

Documentation of instruction; behavioral interventions; academic and behavioral progress; and meetings with parents, support staff, and community resource personnel is a never-ending job. I have often resented the drain on my time, energy, and creativity created by the paperwork avalanche. Although accurate records that support the educational process for a student are legal and ethical necessities, accountability procedures can and must be streamlined. As teachers, our priorities are our students. Managing the monstrous mounds of paper requires some organization. The following suggestions come from my still-evolving strategies for creative, efficient, educationally sound compliance:

1. *Use theme folders, theme planning forms, and daily lesson plan forms that allow for a fill-in-the-blank response.* Once suitable forms are found or developed to meet the needs of a group, time can be saved by using the forms instead of writing the same headings, resource lists, student names, or schedule over and over. I was able to cut my weekly lesson planning time from 3 hours per week to 1 1/2 hours per week by using a self-developed planning form. Using an established format saves time because routine information is already in place. I can put objectives, page numbers, a skeleton list of activities, and an evaluation procedure in place quickly. Later, while showering, driving to and from work, or cooking dinner, I play with ideas for making instruction and learning more exciting and fun. My mind is free to wander and create because the compliance information is in place.

The advantage of having theme planning forms and folders is that more than one unit can be in a planning phase at once. Waiting until one unit of study is completed to begin planning for the next unit of study is deadly. Fatigue, unexpected meetings, scarcity of resource materials, the addition of a new student, unplanned personal demands on time, and possible behavioral upheavals within the group can combine to overwhelm the best intentions.

I plan an overview for no less than a semester at a time. I prefer to plan for the whole year. This overview is broad. It contains a scope and sequence for math, reading, and written language skills; a topic and timeline for instructional themes; and special projects that will support instructional and behavioral goals for the group. This allows for more efficient use of time, money, and energy. It allows me to write minigrant proposals and petition more successfully for in-house funding. Best of all, it allows me to prepare students and their parents for academic and behavioral progress. It allows me to spend the maximum amount of time possible in quality efforts for and with my students.

2. *Keep a "wish list" at all times.* Prioritize the items on the list. Have all ordering information available. When money is made available, the timeline for using it is often short. Having an overall yearly plan and knowing what you want, why you want it, and where to get it will increase the likelihood that your request will be honored.

3. *Integrate individualized education program (IEP) objectives with local, state, and federal guidelines.* Some districts already have a form for this. If this is not required on a formal document, have a checklist available for students, parents, support staff, and other professionals. This checklist can be as simple as the targeted scope and sequence for math, reading, and writing, with IEP objectives for each individual student highlighted.

4. *Keep a weekly grade sheet on a clipboard.* The grade books that are typically issued are too hard to manage in a class for EBD. A sample weekly grade sheet is provided in the Appendix. This form allows you to see what has been completed at a glance. Recording grades each day provides immediate feedback to students and keeps the stacks of ungraded papers from piling up. An associate or the students can average the grades each week and record them on the grade sheet. At the end of a grading period, only the weekly averages will need to be considered. Students like to keep track of their own progress. I usually set aside time each Friday to allow students to average and chart their grades. We then have a group discussion (and sometimes a math lesson) on how students could improve.

5. *Keep line or bar graphs of behavioral points if a point system is being used.* A long string of numbers is usually meaningless to a student, parent, or professional outside the immediate setting. A graph gives an immediate picture of a student's progress. Because it is easier to identify patterns when patterns are present, the graph enhances feedback to students.

   I started keeping bar graphs long before they were required. An affective bulletin board with a positive title and related illustrations would contain each student's bar graph chart for a month. Each day, I would place a line on their charts to indicate the number of points earned. The students would color their charts. At the end of the month, I would photocopy the charts, file the photocopies, and send the originals home with the students with a brief note to the parents. The students loved this as much as their parents. In addition to charting daily progress, I would place a red line across a full week to indicate the targeted number of points each day for that week. Every student would have a different target. The targeted number of points would be 10% more than their average for the previous 2 weeks. This would allow me to individualize reward opportunities but still remain fair in the students' eyes. Everyone had to meet or exceed his or her target.

6. *Along with a record of points (if points are being used), keep anecdotal information in some time-efficient way.* This information can be developed into a checklist with

space at the bottom for a brief narrative statement. These records should be available to you at all times during the day. Waiting until the end of the day or week to fill them out wastes time, and valuable information is often forgotten. When an incident occurs, write the date, time, and people involved immediately. Quickly place check marks next to the items on the form that describe the student's actions. A narrative report can be added later, but do not wait longer than necessary. The form should also include information about contact with a parent or another agency. If none is made, that can be indicated. If contact with others is made, the details should be recorded. The disciplinary action taken is another essential piece of information that should be added to the form. Again, the standard hierarchy of consequences can be listed. All you need to do is check the one taken and record the amount of time the student will be expected to complete if the student is required to be in time out.

7. *Implement a system for recording positive growth beyond simple charting of points.* The incident reports give a clear picture of problem behaviors and the charts illustrate patterns of behavior, but a weekly narrative of positive events is needed to complete the profile. The back of the point graph can be divided into weekly sections. These positive events can be recorded during affective instruction as students discuss successes. Students can be asked to write their own list of accomplishments. You can then add a brief note.

8. *Develop a form for recording telephone and face-to-face conferences.* The form should include a place for a date, who was involved, a brief description of the topics covered, and signatures. Complete the form as you conduct the conference or immediately after the conference. As you may guess, I rarely go anywhere without my clipboard. Those odd minutes waiting in line for lunch, for a faculty meeting to start, or for a bell to ring are too precious to waste.

9. *Have a system in place.* Otherwise, with IEP's, academic checklists, incident reports, point graphs, grades, positive comments, and conference forms, the paperwork can become unmanageable. Establish a notebook (not a folder) for each student. Place subject dividers in each notebook. Have a file folder labeled "To Be Filed." Put all student forms in that folder as soon as they are completed. With a system in place, an associate can place items in the notebooks while the class is involved in an activity that does not require his or her attention.

10. *Before school starts for the year, make an associate's handbook.* Provide the associate with copies of all forms, instructions on where to place them in the student notebooks, and any other information related to instruction and behavior management that he or she needs to know.

11. *Keep a calendar.* Due dates for county and federal paperwork are important. Funding for special programs often rests on these documents. A calendar can help in prioritizing instructional and administrative concerns.

12. *Either put it away, or throw it away!* When it comes to the incredible amount of paper that accumulates, I have learned to keep this rule at work but am still fighting to master it at home. The stacks can become unmanageable too quickly. Part of the secret of managing this less appealing aspect of teaching is to control it rather than having it control you.

The essence of the preceding 12 suggestions can be summed up in two general guidelines: (1) Have a system and (2) follow the system daily. Waiting to complete all incident reports until later in the day or week; hunting for misplaced forms;

being unprepared with documentation for conferences; staying up all night to average grades or write lesson plans; and facing a class of students with EBD tired and stressed is a recipe for burnout. Pace yourself. Organize and simplify the required components. And do not expect to do it all alone.

CONSULTATION

Teachers are being called upon to take a more active role in consultation and collaboration with each other, with parents and guardians, and with outside agencies. While this can take a great deal of time, it is an essential part of the job. When a teacher knows about the strengths and needs of the students, other interested and involved adults are included, and a team approach is implemented, maximum benefits can occur for the students. Following are some general guidelines taken from Turnbull and Turnbull (1990) for facilitating productive working relationships with other adults:

1. Be an active listener. Make comments. Ask questions. Share information. Clearly communicate a willingness to listen, learn, and share in the responsibilities inherent in a team effort.

2. Use nonverbal cues that encourage others to relax and participate. Do not put barriers such as desks between speakers. Keep an appropriate distance. Be close enough to convey interest, but respect personal boundaries. Nod, smile, gesture, and indicate acceptance.

3. Be on time for scheduled meetings.

4. Be clear about the objectives of the meeting.

5. State concerns, expectations, and needs positively.

6. Be prepared with supportive documentation.

7. Be aware of the roles, responsibilities, and limitations of the other participants. Misunderstandings can be avoided if each member of the team knows what each other member can and cannot do.

8. Make only promises that can be kept. If a suggestion is made that either cannot be followed or for specific reasons will not be followed, be sure to communicate that. Once an agreement is made, follow through on all requests in the plan.

Once again, it is important to keep records of all transactions. It is helpful to keep a telephone log for each student. Date, time, person contacted, and results of the call can be recorded on a running ledger. This should be filled out at the time of the call. For face-to-face conferences, a form can be developed that would allow each participant to sign his or her name and identify his or her relationship to the student. The form should also have an area designed for the statement of the objective for the meeting, a brief description of the plan, and the person responsible for implementing each portion of the plan. These conference forms should be kept in the students' notebooks. A section in the student notebooks for conference information is a valuable tool in constructing a chronological overview of interventions, people involved, and progress made.

Once again, the key to efficiency is to plan and organize information. Keeping the class demographic sheet up to date with parent telephone numbers and addresses, emergency contact people and their telephone numbers, and community agency contact people and their telephone numbers saves time. Knowing the who, what, when, where, and how of a meeting will facilitate a smooth and timely resolution. Keeping all documentation in order ensures greater clarity of service delivery.

CONCLUDING COMMENTS

The stresses placed on teachers in classes for students with EBD can take their toll. Teachers need to be proactive with themselves as well as with their students. Beyond a guiding philosophy grounded in research and theory, beyond the organizational skills that enhance time management, and beyond the techniques for effective consultation and collaboration lies a real person, and this real person requires care. Take time every day for something you love. Take time every day to reflect. Take time every day to congratulate yourself on something—even if it is just that you got through the day. Take time every day to either set a new goal or evaluate the journey you are taking with the present goal. The worst kind of burnout occurs when there is nothing new to explore. Teaching students with EBD requires the willingness to dream big while celebrating the tiniest of advances. Rilke (1975, p. 25) expressed an attitude worth adopting: "Be patient toward all that is unsolved in your heart; and try to love the questions themselves . . . ."

Bibliography and References

Albert, L. (1989). *A teacher's guide to cooperative discipline.* Circle Pines, MN: American Guidance Service.

Alberto, P. A., & Troutman, A. C. (1982). *Applied behavior analysis for teachers.* Columbus, OH: Merrill.

Allinder, R. (1993). I think i can; i think i can. *Beyond Behavior, 4*(2), 29.

Bender, W. N. (1992). *Learning disabilities: Characteristics, identification, and teaching strategies.* Boston: Allyn and Bacon.

Bloom, Engelhart, Frost, Hill, & Krathwohl. (1956). *Taxonomy of educational objectives handbook I: Cognitive domain.* New York: David McKay.

Braxton, E. (1993). *Violence within and without: Mental health strategies for treating the African-American child.* St. Petersburg, FL: Juvenile Welfare Board.

Bryngelson, J. (1992). *Reaching and teaching troubled kids: The orchestrated classroom.* Billings, MT: Self Esteem Associates.

Canfield, J. (1986). *Self-esteem in the classroom.* Culver City, CA: Self-Esteem Seminars.

Carberry, H. (1976). How can this child be helped? *Instructor, 85*(5). Taken from H. Goldstein (Ed.), *Readings in emotional and behavioral disorders* (1978, pp. 81–83). CT: Special Learning Corporation.

Carroll, L. (1916). *Alice's adventures in Wonderland* and *Through the looking glass.* Chicago: Rand McNally.

Charles, C. M. (1992). *Building classroom discipline.* New York: Longman.

Curwin, R. L., & Mendler, A. N. (1988). *Discipline with dignity.* Alexandria, VA: Association for Supervision and Curriculum Development.

DeBruyn, R. L., & Larson, J. L. (1984). *You can handle them all.* Manhattan, KS: The MASTER Teacher.

Driekurs, R., Grumwald, B. B., & Pepper, F. C. (1982). *Maintaining sanity in the classroom: Classroom management techniques* (2nd ed.). New York: Harper & Row, Publishers.

Ellis, A. (1980). An overview of the clinical theory of rational-emotive therapy. In R. Grieger & J. Byrd (Eds.), *Rational-emotive therapy: A skill-based approach.* New York: Van Nostrand.

Erikson, E. (1950). *Childhood and society.* New York: W. W. Norton.

Fagen, S. (1981). Conducting an LSI: A process model. *The Pointer, 25*(2), 9–11.

Friedenburg, E. Z. (1992, July). Quotable quotes. *Reader's Digest,* p. 137.

Glasow, A. H. (1993, May). Quotable quotes. *Reader's Digest,* p. 33.

Glasser, W. (1985). *Control theory in the classroom.* New York: Perennial Library.

Gleason, M. (1991). Cumulative versus rapid introduction of new information. *Exceptional Children, 57*(4), 353–358.

Gleason, N. (1992). *Proverbs from around the world.* New York: Citadel.

Goldstein, A. (1988). *The prepare curriculum.* Champaign, IL: Research Press.

Guetzloe, E. C. (n.d.[a]). *Management of disruptive or disturbed students.* Unpublished manuscript.

Guetzloe, E. C. (n.d.[b]). *Maslow's hierarchy of needs theory of human motivation.* Unpublished manuscript.

Guetzloe, E. C. (n.d.[c]). *Classroom interventions for children with attention deficit disorders.* Unpublished manuscript.

Heshusius, L. (1991). Curriculum-based assessment and direct instruction: Critical reflections on fundamental assumptions. *Exceptional Children, 57*(4), 315–328.

Heuchart, C., & Long, N. (1981). A brief history of life space interviewing. *The Pointer, 25*(2), 5–8.

Hewett, F. M., & Taylor, F. D. (1980). *The emotionally disturbed child in the classroom: The orchestration of success* (2nd ed.). Boston: Allyn and Bacon.

Hobbs, N. (1982). *The troubled and troubling child.* San Francisco: Jossey-Bass.

Irving, O., & Martin, J. (1982). Withitness: The confusing variable. *American Educational Research Journal, 19,* 313–319.

Kerr, R. (1987). *Positively! Learning to manage negative emotions.* Portland, ME: J. Weston Walch.

Kohler, F. W., Richardson, T., Mina, C., Dinwiddie, G., & Greenwood, C. (1985). Establishing cooperative peer relations in the classroom. *The Pointer, 29*(4), 12–16.

Kounin, J. (1977). *Discipline and group management in classrooms.* New York: Holt, Rinehart and Winston.

Krathwohl, D. R., Bloom, B. S., & Masia, B. B. (1956). *Taxonomy of educational objectives handbook II: Affective domain.* New York: David McKay.

Lewis, C. S. (1956). *Surprised by joy.* Orlando, FL: Harcourt Brace Jovanovich.

Mannix, D. (1993). *Social skills activities for special children.* West Nyack, NY: The Center for Applied Research in Education.

Maslow, A. (1962). *Toward a psychology of being.* Princeton, NJ: Van Nostrand.

McIntyre, T. (1989). *The behavior management book.* Boston: Allyn and Bacon.

Morgan, S. R., & Reinhart, J. A. (1991). *Interventions for students with emotional disorders.* Austin, TX: Pro-Ed.

Piaget, J. (1954, as cited in Woolfolk, 1990). *Educational psychology.* Englewood Cliffs, NJ: Prentice-Hall.

Redl, F. (1966). *When we deal with children.* New York: Free Press.

Redl, F., & Wineman, D. (1965). *Controls from within: Techniques for the treatment of the aggressive child.* New York: Free Press.

Rhodes, W. C. (1965). Curriculum and disordered behavior. In J. Long, W. C. Morse, & R. G. Newman (Eds.), *Conflict in the classroom* (pp. 405–410). Belmont, CA: Wadsworth.

Rilke, R. M. (1975). *Rilke on love and other difficulties.* (Trans. by John J. L. Mood). New York: W. W. Norton.

Rockwell, S. (1993). *Tough to reach, tough to teach: Students with behavior problems.* Reston, VA: The Council for Exceptional Children.

Schurr, S. L. (1989). *Dynamite in the classroom: A how-to book for teachers.* Tampa, FL: The National Resource Center for Middle Grades/High School Education.

Seligman, M. E. P. (1991). *Learned optimism.* New York: Knopf.

Selman, R. L. (1981). The development of interpersonal competence: The role of understanding in conduct. *Developmental Review, 1,* 419.

Slavin, R. E. (1990). *Cooperative learning theory, research, and practice.* Englewood Cliffs, NJ: Prentice-Hall.

Sprick, R. (1981). *The solution book.* Chicago: Science Research Associates.

Sulzer-Azaroff, B., & Mayer, R. G. (1986). *Achieving educational excellence.* New York: Holt, Rinehart, and Winston.

Swap, S. (1974). Disturbing classroom behaviors: A developmental and ecological view. *Exceptional Children, 41*(3). Taken from H. Goldstein (Ed.), *Readings in emotional and behavioral disorders* (1978, pp. 43–50). Guilford, CT: Special Learning Corporation.

Tuckman, B. W. (1965). Developmental sequences in small groups. *Psychological Bulletin, 63,* 384–399.

Turnbull, A. P., & Turnbull, H. R. (1990). *Families, professionals, and exceptionality: A special partnership* (2nd ed.). New York: Merrill.

Vernon, A. (1989a). *Thinking, feeling, behaving, grades 1–6.* Champaign, IL: Research Press.

Vernon, A. (1989b). *Thinking, feeling, behaving, grades 7–12.* Champaign, IL: Research Press.

White, T. H. (1939). *The once and future king.* New York: Ace Books.

Williams, M. (1983). *The velveteen rabbit.* Garden City, NY: Doubleday.

Wood, M. M., Comlos, C., Gunn, A., & Weller, D. (1986). *Developmental therapy in the classroom.* Austin, TX: Pro-Ed.

Yeltsin, B. (1992, April). Quotable quotes. *Reader's Digest,* p. 203.

Appendixes

Affective Instructional Resources

Reinforcement Activities for Stages One, Two, and Three

Behavior Management Planning Forms

Academic Instructional Resources

Instructional Planning Forms

Stage One Theme: Sports

Stage Two Theme: Plants

Stage Three Theme: Economics

Note: The lists of instructional resources are specifically focused to meet both student needs and the budget constraints of most classroom teachers. If money were plentiful, a great deal of technology would be included in the lists of suggested materials. Resources listed are effective and affordable.

AFFECTIVE INSTRUCTIONAL RESOURCES

ELEMENTARY LEVEL

Canfield, J. (1986). *Self-Esteem in the Classroom*

Mannix, D. (1993). *Social Skills Activities for Special Children*

Sprick, R. (1981). *The Solution Book*

Vernon, A. (1989). *Thinking, Feeling, Behaving, Grades 1–6*

DUSO: Developing Understanding of Self and Others (Kits are available for grades K–2 and 3–4.)

TAD: Toward Affective Development (Kits meet the needs of students in grades 3–6.)

MIDDLE SCHOOL AND HIGH SCHOOL LEVEL

Canfield, J. (1986). *Self-Esteem in the Classroom*

DeBruyn, R. L., & Larson, J. L. (1984). *You Can Handle Them All*

Goldstein, A. (1988). *The Prepare Curriculum*

Kerr, R. (1987). *Positively! Learning to Manage Negative Emotions*

Vernon, A. (1989). *Thinking, Feeling, Behaving, Grades 7–12*

Materials developed to teach conflict resolution and peer mediation skills are especially important for this age group as well.

REINFORCEMENT ACTIVITIES FOR
STAGES ONE, TWO, AND THREE

STAGE ONE REINFORCEMENT ACTIVITIES

1. Allow students to earn time to use the computer for games that will increase their basic knowledge level of proficiency or to type stories and poems for a class anthology or newspaper.

2. Have matching games available that can be used by individuals initially. As students become ready, two at a time may begin to play Concentration-type games together.

3. Have a variety of art materials available. Students can draw, build dioramas to illustrate a topic of study, or trace and cut items for a group bulletin board.

4. Construct or purchase a variety of Bingo- and Jeopardy-type games that include facts being learned in class. Students can play these games as a whole group.

5. Make drills of basic skills more motivating by having a weekly "Inside Olympics" event. Set up a table, desk, section of the chalkboard, or bulletin board with a task for each student. Students will work independently at each task for a predetermined amount of time. As a signal is given, students will rotate to the next activity. This process is repeated until each student has participated in each event. Students carry an Inside Olympics Score Card with them to record their answers for each task. Score cards are checked and tallied. All students who achieve appropriate levels receive a reward. Some ideas for Inside Olympic events include the following:

   - Have students pitch 10 pennies on a mat that has numbers placed in squares. Students can add, subtract, multiply, or divide the numbers as teacher directions indicate.

   - Put a tape recorder in one center with 10 words recorded on it. Have these words placed on cards in random order on the desk. Students must listen to the words on the tape and place them in the correct order. Students then write the words.

   - At the next station, scatter definition cards that match the words given on the tape in random order. Students must match the definition cards with the words and write the definitions next to the words on the score card.

   - Another station may contain a series of pictures that have been shuffled. Students must put them in sequential order. A good source for this type of activity is the newspaper comics.

   - Have students put word cards in alphabetical order and then copy them.

   - Have students place word and/or picture cards in categories and then copy them.

   - Have students unscramble words.

   - Have students unscramble sentence strips.

   - Have students match beginnings of sentences with endings.

BOOK BINDING WITH PLASTIC ADHESIVE

1. **Collate and staple pages to be bound.**

2. **Cut 2 pieces of poster board slightly larger than the pages of the book.**

3. **Cut the plastic adhesive 1"–2" larger than the front and back covers made of poster board.**

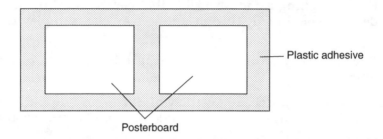

Plastic adhesive

Posterboard

4. **Peel the paper off the plastic. Place the poster board on the adhesive side of the plastic as shown in the diagram. The space between the 2 pieces of poster board should be wide enough to accommodate the inside pages of the book when the covers are closed.**

5. **Fold the corners of the plastic down first. Then fold the edges as shown.**

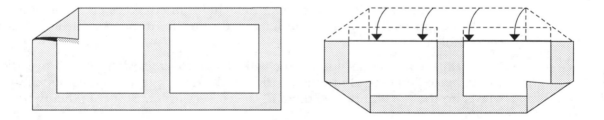

6. **Place the stapled pages on the back cover. Cut plastic adhesive to fit the inside front cover and the cover page of the inside of the book.**

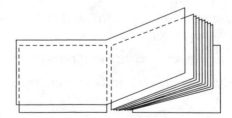

7. **Turn the book to the back cover and repeat Step 6.**

8. **Decorate the front of the book as desired.**

Source: *Back Off, Cool Down, Try Again*, Sylvia Rockwell, 1995, Reston, VA: The Council for Exceptional Children.

- Have students construct puzzles.

- Have students write riddles about science or social studies facts. They can record their answers on the score card.

Cut-and-paste activities can replace the copying portions of the tasks if students are reluctant to write.

6. A variation on the Inside Olympics game is a Scavenger Hunt. This can be done at each student's desk by asking a variety of questions that will require the student to use his or her textbooks to find the answers. This is a good activity for students who need practice making inferences about the type of resource to use.

7. Do simple cooking activities that allow each student to work independently. The whole group can participate at the same time as long as the need for interaction is kept to a minimum or is closely monitored by an adult.

8. Have students make an alphabet book or a puppet play for a younger class.

The key to success during Stage One is having fun in ways that do not over stimulate students who are not ready to function as friends. Opportunities for sharing, taking turns, and interactions must be planned carefully and increased slowly.

STAGE TWO REINFORCEMENT ACTIVITIES

1. Begin to allow students to work in pairs. Teach them to take responsibility for team efforts by giving each person a specific task. Examples include the following:

   - Practice spelling words or math facts. One person acts as a tutor for a period of time and then roles are switched for an equal period of time.

   - Proofread written material. Each partner checks the work of his or her partner with a different color pen.

   - Write paragraphs after completing Venn diagrams about information that each person has contributed. Once again, partners can add their parts to a Venn diagram in a different color pen or pencil.

2. Provide games that two people can play together such as Concentration, card games, or computer games.

3. Set up Inside Olympics or a Scavenger Hunt that partners can work together to complete.

4. Develop group-produced radio plays. Record these on a tape recorder. A few students can make sound effects; others can be actors and actresses. This is a good transitional activity because it does not require students to act on a stage. Reading becomes much more enjoyable with this format.

5. Develop presentations that require each student to contribute a part without interacting with others. An example of this would be the recitation of a poem that has clearly delineated sections.

6. Plan a group activity that includes other adults in the school. Students can cook a few of their favorite snacks, write invitations, and practice the social skills needed for welcoming visitors to the classroom. This is especially reinforcing near holidays or after the group has completed a unit of study and has displays of work to share.

7. Make a television box by cutting a screen-sized hole in the side of a cardboard box. Use cardboard tubes for rollers. Make a class version of a common story or song. Have each member of the class illustrate a section of the story or song. Place these in order on a long piece of butcher paper. Roll the illustrated story or song on the tubes. Position the tubes in the box. Have one student roll the illustration while the others sing or take turns reciting sections of the story for other classes.

The key to success during Stage Two is building cooperative efforts between students in nonthreatening ways. Be prepared to have the class return to independent activities if the students show signs of needing increased structure by exhibiting more frequent problems.

STAGE THREE REINFORCEMENT ACTIVITIES

During Stage Three any age-appropriate activity can be managed. Stage Three activities should encourage the generalization of skills learned in previous stages. For this to occur, the teacher must remain available and supportive without hovering too closely. Students should be allowed to settle minor differences on their own. Another important aspect of activities during this stage is the introduction of unfamiliar adults and students into the classroom as well as opportunities to practice skills in other settings. Field trips, guest speakers, and increased involvement with classes in regular education settings make the transition from a self-contained, protected environment to the mainstream less stressful.

Cooperative ventures with other classes are excellent ways to build student confidence. Plan academic tournaments, debates, poster presentations, plays, or cultural events that require more than one class to work together. Teach students to promote a positive image of themselves by saying "Hello" when they see others in the hall, displaying their work in the media center, and entering school-wide events. My classes have participated in county-wide events as well. They have competed against regular education and gifted classes. One of my elementary classes wrote a puppet play and made a videotape of it. They earned honors-level ribbons in the county media festival. A middle school class completed the economics unit included in this book, ran a minibusiness making and selling peanut butter candy, and videotaped sample job interviews to demonstrate appropriate and inappropriate interviewing behavior. They kept ledgers of business expenses and profits and made a large bulletin board display of key vocabulary, business growth charts, and other important things they had learned. The work was clearly done by students. It was neat and legible, but it did not look as professional or polished as some of the other economics fair entries. We were proud to discover that our class had earned second place county wide in the competition's middle school display division.

Having the teacher's support is an important first step. When students reach Stage Three, they are ready to spread their wings, and the teacher must be ready to let them go. During Stage One, the teacher is out in front as the primary leader. During Stage Two, the teacher begins to bring the students to his or her side as partners in a shared process of growth. By Stage Three, some of the students in the class should be ready to take leadership roles in the room, in the school, and possibly even in county-wide events. If our students are going to be ready to meet the demands of an increasingly complex society, we have to show them that they are ready with proof that extends beyond the walls of the classroom—and then we have to trust them. We have to say, "You can do it!" and really mean it.

In closing, I'd like to share one more story from personal experience with an extremely aggressive group of fifth graders. These boys had all witnessed the violent deaths of family members or friends and lived in a crack-infested section of the city. They did not believe in their ability to do more than fight. I worked hard to convince them that violence was not necessary and was not to be tolerated in the classroom. Then I slaved to teach them that they were bright and capable students. We suffered through many threats, temper tantrums, and stubborn acts of defiance, but finally the group began to settle down. It became a group of functioning, caring, productive people.

During Teacher Appreciation Week, the social worker decided to tape record students' responses to the question, "Why do you like your teacher?" As these messages were played over the intercom during morning announcements, I heard students in other classes say such things as, "My teacher is nice. She gives us candy." I smiled at their childish evaluations and thought about how much I had liked a family friend when I was young for the same reason. Then one of my boys introduced himself and said, "I like Mrs. Rockwell because she doesn't want to hear about what we can't do. She wants to know what we *can* do."

Public demonstrations of emotion are not my style. I'd rather be ill than cry in front of people. But that day I had to stop what I was doing to blow my nose. That student gave me one of my most cherished memories as a teacher. My greatest desire is that every child who passes through our doors will leave with the knowledge of what is right, strong, good, and possible about his or her behavior and abilities.

Make Stage Three count. It is easy to get complacent when things are going well. Other teachers and supervisors will question the placement of the students. They certainly will not behave as though they have severe problems. However, students will not automatically transfer their new skills to other settings and people without opportunities to test the waters near the safety of the shore first. Make sure they know they can do it alone before asking them to be on their own 100% of the time.

BEHAVIOR MANAGEMENT PLANNING FORMS

INCIDENT REPORT FORM

Student's Name _____   Date _____

Teacher _____   Room _____

_____ Refusing to work	_____ Destroying property
_____ Throwing items	_____ Talking without permission
_____ Disrupting with noises	_____ Using inappropriate language
_____ Teasing classmates	_____ Refusing to follow directions
_____ Moving out of assigned area	_____ Making inappropriate gestures
_____ Sleeping	_____ Using physical aggression
_____ Employing excessive and inappropriate attention-seeking behaviors	

Supporting Details _____

_____

_____

_____

_____

Actions Taken _____

_____

_____

_____

_____

Outcomes _____

_____

_____

_____

_____

Source: *Back Off, Cool Down, Try Again*, Sylvia Rockwell, 1995, Reston, VA: The Council for Exceptional Children.

TELEPHONE LOG

Student _____

Date	Contact Person	Issues Discussed
_____	_____	_____
_____	_____	_____
_____	_____	_____
_____	_____	_____
_____	_____	_____
_____	_____	_____
_____	_____	_____
_____	_____	_____
_____	_____	_____
_____	_____	_____
_____	_____	_____
_____	_____	_____
_____	_____	_____
_____	_____	_____
_____	_____	_____
_____	_____	_____
_____	_____	_____

Source: *Back Off, Cool Down, Try Again*, Sylvia Rockwell, 1995, Reston, VA: The Council for Exceptional Children.

CONFERENCE DOCUMENTATION

Date _____

Issues Discussed _____

_____

_____

_____

Actions Taken	Person(s) Responsible
_____	_____
_____	_____
_____	_____
_____	_____
_____	_____
_____	_____
_____	_____
_____	_____

Signature	Title
_____	_____
_____	_____
_____	_____
_____	_____
_____	_____
_____	_____

Source: *Back Off, Cool Down, Try Again*, Sylvia Rockwell, 1995, Reston, VA: The Council for Exceptional Children.

CLASS PROFILE SHEET

Student's Name	Age	Date of Birth	Grade	Morph-ology	IQ	Reading Level	Math Level	Placement Behaviors

Source: *Back Off, Cool Down, Try Again*, Sylvia Rockwell, 1995, Reston, VA: The Council for Exceptional Children.

GROUP DEMOGRAPHIC CHART

Student's Name	Parent's Name and Telephone Number	Student's Address	Emergency Contact's Name, Telephone Number, and Address	Other Agency Contacts' Telephone Numbers	IEP and Reevaluation Dates

Source: *Back Off, Cool Down, Try Again*, Sylvia Rockwell, 1995, Reston, VA: The Council for Exceptional Children.

WEEKLY POINT SHEET

	Mon	Tues	Wed	Thurs	Fri
100					
90					
80					
70					
60					
50					
40					
30					
20					
10					

Daily
Score _____ _____ _____ _____ _____

Week of _____

	Mon	Tues	Wed	Thurs	Fri
100					
90					
80					
70					
60					
50					
40					
30					
20					
10					

Daily
Score _____ _____ _____ _____ _____

Week of _____

	Mon	Tues	Wed	Thurs	Fri
100					
90					
80					
70					
60					
50					
40					
30					
20					
10					

Daily
Score _____ _____ _____ _____ _____

Week of _____

	Mon	Tues	Wed	Thurs	Fri
100					
90					
80					
70					
60					
50					
40					
30					
20					
10					

Daily
Score _____ _____ _____ _____ _____

Week of _____

Source: *Back Off, Cool Down, Try Again*, Sylvia Rockwell, 1995, Reston, VA: The Council for Exceptional Children.

Problem Solving Sheet

1. What was the problem? _____

_____

2. When? _____

Where? _____

With whom? _____

_____

3. What positive choices could you have made?

_____

_____

_____

4. What will you earn? _____

_____

Source: *Back Off, Cool Down, Try Again*, Sylvia Rockwell, 1995, Reston, VA: The Council for Exceptional Children.

DECISION-MAKING SHEET

Name _____

Date _____

1. **What was happening before the problem occurred?** _____

   _____

   _____

2. **What was your behavior when the problem began?** _____

   _____

   _____

3. **How did you feel?** _____

4. **What other things could you have done? Name at least four that would have been more appropriate.** _____

   _____

   _____

   _____

   _____

5. **Which one of the four behaviors you listed in question 4 would you like best?**

   _____

   Why would your prefer to do that? _____

   _____

   What would you have earned if you had chosen that behavior instead of the one you described in question 2? _____

   _____

6. **What has the problem behavior earned for you?** _____

   _____

7. **How are you feeling now?** _____

   _____

8. **Did you make any good decisions in spite of the problem? What were they?**

   _____

   _____

9. **What can you do now to help yourself have a good day?** _____

   _____

   _____

Source: *Back Off, Cool Down, Try Again*, Sylvia Rockwell, 1995, Reston, VA: The Council for Exceptional Children.

BLANK CONTRACT

1. Problem Behaviors

2. Desired Behavior

3. Punishments

4. Rewards

5. Signatures

Student _____

Teacher _____

Any Other Staff Member(s) Involved _____

Source: *Back Off, Cool Down, Try Again*, Sylvia Rockwell, 1995, Reston, VA: The Council for Exceptional Children.

ACADEMIC INSTRUCTIONAL RESOURCES

When planning integrated, thematic instructional units, it is important to use resources already available. This saves time and money. The two companies listed below, however, have developed a variety of units that are flexible enough to meet the needs of students on many grade levels. These units are literature based and highly motivational. To receive complete listings of unit topics, write to the addresses or call the telephone numbers provided. These inexpensive units can save teachers valuable time and money. A few of the topics that are available include Insects, Ecology, Civil War, Transcontinental Railroad, The Human Body, and Weather. There are too many to mention in this publication. Each of the units I have used has been of high quality.

Creative Teaching Press, Inc. (CTP)
Cypress, CA 90630

Book Cooks: Grades K–3
Book Cooks: Grades 4–6

(Both cookbooks are literature based and published by CTP.)

Evan-Moor Corporation
8 Lower Ragsdale Drive
Monterey, CA 93940-5746
800/777-4362

Teacher Created Materials, Inc.
P. O. Box 1214
Huntington Beach, CA 92647

Other resources for instructional support materials include the following businesses and organizations that provide games, posters, and miniunits at little or no cost to teachers:

Environmental Jeopardy Game ($5.00)
Mindy Maslin
The Pennsylvania Horticulture Society
325 Walnut Street
Philadelphia, PA 19106-2777

Multicultural History: The Potato
Washington State Potato Commission
108 Interlake Road
Moses Lake, WA 98837

National Live Stock and Meat Board
444 North Michigan Avenue
Chicago, IL 60611

The National Live Stock and Meat Board provides complete classroom instructional packets on a variety of food-related topics for kindergarten through secondary school. The packets include vocabulary lists, lesson plans, worksheets, enrichment activity suggestions, and colorful bulletin board materials. Prices range from $1.50 to $8.00.

RESOURCES FOR MULTICULTURAL UNITS

The following books provide literature-based instructional units on a variety of cultural topics. The materials can be combined with science, social studies, reading, math, and art lessons to broaden students' appreciation and understanding of other cultures. Another option for their use would be concentrated units of study on particular cultures in isolation. Both approaches can be used throughout the year depending on the needs of the group.

Connecting Holidays & Literature
Teacher Created Materials
P. O. Box 1214
Huntington Beach, CA 92647

Connecting Cultures & Literature
Teacher Created Materials
P. O. Box 1214
Huntington Beach, CA 92647

Native American and Multicultural Folk Tales Thematic Units
Teacher Created Materials
P. O. Box 1214
Huntington Beach, CA 92647

INSTRUCTIONAL PLANNING FORMS

ABBREVIATIONS LIST FOR LESSON PLANS

DOPS	Daily Oral Problem Solving
DOW	Daily Oral Writing
DVE	Daily Vocabulary Enrichment
Exp	Experiment
IP	Independent Practice
P	Page
PD	Participation in Discussion
pp	Pages
RA	Read Aloud
Sp	Spelling
SP	Student Product
TDL	Teacher-Directed Lesson
TM	Teacher's Manual
TMM	Teacher-Made Materials
TO	Teacher Observation
TT	Timed Test
w/	With
Wds	Words
Wksht	Worksheet
w/o	Without

For Group Lessons:

DGOPS	Daily whole-group problem-solving practice
DGOW	Daily whole-group proofreading practice
DGVE	Daily whole-group discussion of a selected word

Source: Rockwell (1993), p. 62.

SAMPLE LESSON PLAN FORMAT

_____   _____   Week of _____
    (Teacher)   (School)

_____   _____
    (Subject)   (Time)

Group I. _____   Book _____

    _____

    (Names of Students)

Group II. _____

    _____

    _____

    (Names of Students)

Daily Activities:

TT on Individual Facts DGOPS found in book _____ on p. _____

Monday: Group I.   Objectives _____
                          TDL/TM p. _____   Assignment/p. _____
                          Evaluation Method _____

              Group II.   Objectives _____
                          TDL/TM p. _____   Assignment/p. _____
                          Evaluation Method _____

Tuesday: Group I.   Objectives _____
                           TDL/TM p. _____   Assignment/p. _____
                          Evaluation Method _____

              Group II.   Objectives _____
                          TDL/TM p. _____   Assignment/p. _____
                          Evaluation Method _____

Wednesday: Group I.   Objectives _____
                           TDL/TM p. _____   Assignment/p. _____
                          Evaluation Method _____

              Group II.   Objectives _____
                          TDL/TM p. _____   Assignment/p. _____
                          Evaluation Method _____

Thursday: Group I.   Objectives _____
                           TDL/TM p. _____   Assignment/p. _____
                          Evaluation Method _____

              Group II.   Objectives _____
                          TDL/TM p. _____   Assignment/p. _____
                          Evaluation Method _____

Friday: Group I.   Objectives _____
                           TDL/TM p. _____   Assignment/p. _____
                          Evaluation Method _____

              Group II.   Objectives _____
                          TDL/TM p. _____   Assignment/p. _____
                          Evaluation Method _____

Source: *Back Off, Cool Down, Try Again*, Sylvia Rockwell, 1995, Reston, VA: The Council for Exceptional Children.

WEEKLY GRADE SHEET

Week of _____

Student's Name	Math					Reading					Language/ Spelling					Science/Health					Social Studies				
	M	T	W	R	F	M	T	W	R	F	M	T	W	R	F	M	T	W	R	F	M	T	W	R	F

Source: *Back Off, Cool Down, Try Again*, Sylvia Rockwell, 1995, Reston, VA: The Council for Exceptional Children.

GRAPH OF TEST SCORES

Name _____

Starting Date _____

Mastery Date _____

Set _____

Math facts or vocabulary could be placed on the "Items to Be Mastered" lines. Periodic test scores could be recorded on the graph.

Items to Be Mastered

25
24
23
22
21
20
19
18
17
16
15
14
13
12
11
10
9
8
7
6
5
4
3
2
1
0

Test Dates

Source: *Back Off, Cool Down, Try Again*, Sylvia Rockwell, 1995, Reston, VA: The Council for Exceptional Children.

UNIT PLANNING SHEET

Date/Literature

Reading / Language Arts / Math / Science/Social Studies | Reading / Language Arts / Math / Science/Social Studies

Mon.
Tues.
Wed.
Thurs.
Fri.

Date/Literature

Reading / Language Arts / Math / Science/Social Studies | Reading / Language Arts / Math / Science/Social Studies

Mon.
Tues.
Wed.
Thurs.
Fri.

Date/Literature

Reading / Language Arts / Math / Science/Social Studies | Reading / Language Arts / Math / Science/Social Studies

Mon.
Tues.
Wed.
Thurs.
Fri.

Date/Literature

Reading / Language Arts / Math / Science/Social Studies | Reading / Language Arts / Math / Science/Social Studies

Mon.
Tues.
Wed.
Thurs.
Fri.

Source: *Back Off, Cool Down, Try Again*, Sylvia Rockwell, 1995, Reston, VA: The Council for Exceptional Children.

SEMESTER PLANS

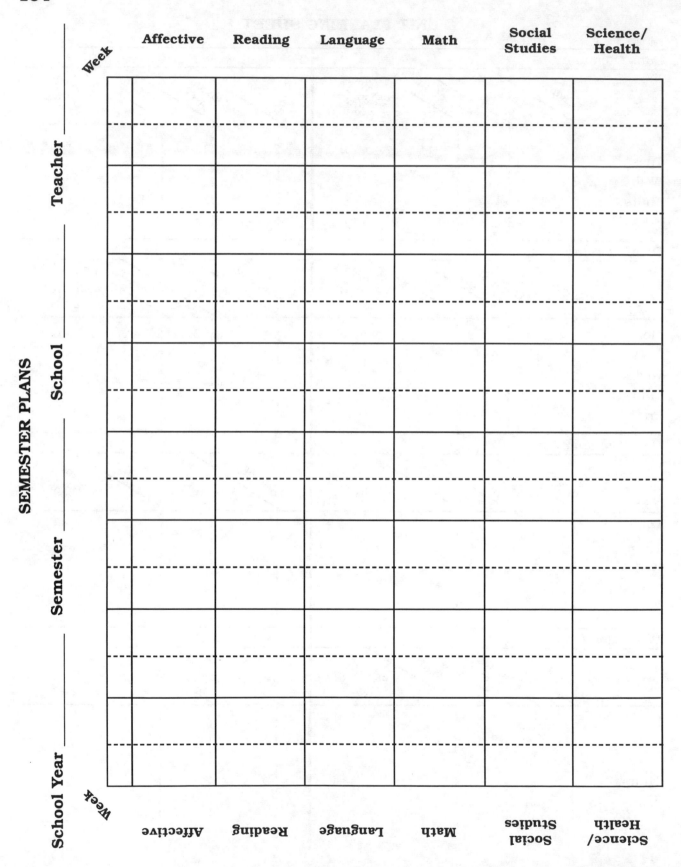

Week	Affective	Reading	Language	Math	Social Studies	Science/ Health

Source: *Back Off, Cool Down, Try Again*, Sylvia Rockwell, 1995, Reston, VA: The Council for Exceptional Children.

STAGE ONE THEME: SPORTS

Starting the year with a sports theme has many advantages. Most students have an interest in one or more sports; a variety of materials is available on many different reading levels; and the affective issues of a new group of students can be addressed in a nonthreatening, age-appropriate manner. One of the goals of Stage One group management is to encourage personal achievement and responsibility within the context of a sense of belonging. Precision teaching and direct instruction can be used to build a solid base of knowledge-level information for use in higher functioning collaborative efforts requiring application, synthesis, and evaluation.

An overview of a 5-week unit plan is provided. Targeted skills can be adjusted to meet the needs of students at lower and higher functioning levels. A narrative description of appropriate Stage One lessons and activities as well as a list of possible resources is included. When planning for this initial stage of group development, keep the need for interaction between students to a minimum, provide ample opportunities for success, encourage adult-to-student involvement, and promote a shift from egocentric pursuits to group affiliation.

WEEK 1

Affective Bulletin Board

Make a bulletin board background that looks like a football field, basketball court, or some other setting for a locally popular sports event. Place a few large, colorful players near the goals. In large letters above the illustrations place the words, "Make That Goal!" Have a hundred or more balls precut. As students exhibit appropriate behaviors, write their names on the balls with a brief description of the positive choice made. Scatter the balls around the playing area of the bulletin board display. Students like the recognition. Within a few days, even the older students begin to check the bulletin board for their names. A positive competition tends to develop. Students compete for good behaviors instead of negative, attention-seeking behaviors.

Reading and Language Arts

Newspaper articles are the most inexpensive and readily available resources for any classroom. A variety of activities can be adapted to meet the needs of students during independent work periods. The class can read sports articles and answer Who, What, When, Where, Why, and How questions. This can lead to a discussion of interviewing and reporting skills. Adults from the school can be invited into the class to be interviewed by individual students. A prepared set of questions can be developed prior to the interviewing session. Each student would be responsible for talking with one adult, recording the information gathered (with that adult's assistance if needed), writing an article, and presenting it for publication in a class newspaper or book.

Math

Place value and numeration skills are usually found at the beginning of published math textbooks. These skills can be adapted to include sports trivia, yard-line dimensions, scoring, players per team, and other related topics.

Science

Science is a personal favorite. Experiments and demonstrations are worth their weight in gold for interest-boosting power and guaranteed success. After exploring basic properties of air, Boyle's Law, Charles' Law, and the Bernoulli Principle are great places to start in understanding what makes a basketball bounce.

To demonstrate that air takes up space, blow up a beach ball. Then show that air has weight by placing a deflated beach ball on one side of a balance and an inflated beach ball on the other side. To prove that both beach balls weigh the same amount without air in them, place them on opposite sides of the balance before inflating one of them.

Boyle's Law. Boyle's Law states that the volume of a container is related to the amount of air pressure exhibited. A container with less volume will contain greater pressure than a container with more volume given the same amount of air. To show this, use a basketball and a smaller inflatable ball. With a manual pump, give both balls one shot of air. Let each student squeeze each ball. The smaller one will have the most pressure.

Charles' Law. Charles' Law states that an increase in temperature will increase air pressure. A decrease in temperature will decrease air pressure. This can be demonstrated by placing a deflated balloon over the opening of a glass bottle. Place the bottle in a pan of boiling water. The heated air will rise and expand, filling the balloon. When the bottle is placed in a pan of cold water, the air will contract and the balloon will deflate.

Bernoulli's Principle. Bernoulli's Principle states that the faster air moves, the less pressure is exerted. This is the reason why golf balls have dimples in them and why footballs are shaped the way they are. To demonstrate this phenomenon, use a handheld hair dryer and a Ping Pong ball. Turn the hair dryer on high, pointing the stream of air toward the ceiling. Place the Ping Pong ball in the stream of air. Once the ball is stabilized in the stream of air, begin to tilt the hair dryer to the side at an angle. The Ping Pong ball will appear to float like magic in the stream of air. The moving air has less pressure than the still air on either side. That is why the Ping Pong ball is not pulled to earth by gravity.

Another way to demonstrate this is to use apples suspended by string. Hang the apples so they are about an inch apart. Blow swiftly between them. They will bounce into each other as if pulled by a magnetic force. The moving air between them has less pressure than the air on either side so the air on the sides exerts pressure and forces them together. Students can draw and label the experiments, write narrative descriptions of the events, sequence sentence strips, or match words with definitions.

Social Studies

The Sports unit lends itself well to a study of states or countries. If the Olympics are in session, a world map can be displayed. Students can decorate flags for each country and place them on the map, construct dioramas depicting cultural scenes, and write reports. If students are learning about the United States, they can use trading cards. They can memorize each state's team, flag, capitol, and placement on the map. Learning to identify states and their capitols is easier if the country is divided into regions. Regional geography, climate, foods, literature, music, and history can be explored as well.

WEEK 2

Reading and Language Arts

Magazine articles can be used as resources for teaching main idea and supporting details. Mobiles can be constructed with the main ideas printed in bold letters at the top and the supporting details written on 3" x 5" cards and hanging by yarn in order of importance. Interviews from Week 1 can be typed into a computer and printed to make a class newspaper or magazine. Naming the periodical, deciding on the frequency of publication, and designing illustrations are ways to help individuals establish positive personal outlets for membership in a group effort.

Math

Whole number operations can be adapted at various levels to incorporate skills students need to learn and sports-related material.

Science

There are four forces that act upon objects in flight: thrust, drag, lift, and gravity. Students can test the aerodynamic qualities of different sizes and shapes of balls. A slingshot or heavy rubber tubing mounted on a sturdy piece of wood can be drawn back a predetermined distance to provide the same amount of thrust to each object. Students can then measure the distance traveled by each ball to determine its aerodynamic capabilities.

Social Studies

Continue with the study of countries or states begun during Week 1.

WEEKS 3 AND 4

Affective Bulletin Board

Use the qualities necessary for success in sports as a way to foster appropriate class participation. Make a bulletin board titled "What Does It Take to Be an Athlete?" As students read about their favorite athletes, generate a list of qualities such as attention to detail, commitment to the team, willingness to practice, and the like. Discuss how these qualities relate to school and job success. Provide each student with a checklist generated by the class. Have students rate themselves on their sportsmanship quotient.

Reading and Language Arts

After a look at current events in sports, students can gain some historical perspective by reading biographies of famous athletes. A company called Creative Education, Inc., located at 123 South Broad Street in Mankata, Minnesota, 56001, publishes a series of biographies of famous athletes and histories of national teams. Students can read these and construct timelines. These timelines can be used to teach summarization and outlining skills.

Math

A study of whole-number operations can continue during Week 3. By Week 4, the class can begin to look at the measurement of time. Students can arrange vocabulary words such as *decade*, *century*, *year*, *month*, *week*, *day*, *hour*, and *second* in order from smallest to largest. They can examine time keeping in sports events. They can name and explain time zones across the United States or the world. They can use stop watches to time individuals doing teacher-selected tasks. Charts can be kept to check for improvements. The study of time can be extended into Week 5.

Science

Begin the study of the human body. This can develop into another group-building activity for younger students by having them create life-sized outlines of themselves. One side can be decorated to look like the student, the other side can be used to display organs of the various systems studied during Weeks 3, 4, and 5. Student bodies can be displayed on the walls of the classroom or just outside the door to introduce the group to people passing by.

Social Studies

Proceed with the study of countries or states as outlined in Week 1.

WEEK 5

Reading and Language Arts

Explore various careers connected with sports. The athletes make up only a small fraction of the people involved. Have each student decide on a possible career and write a description of it. Plan a culminating activity for this unit on sports by making a Jeopardy-type question-and-answer game that covers all the categories of information presented in all subject areas. Use a portion of each reading and language arts period to conduct rapid-fire drills of trivia and vocabulary that will be used during the Sports Tournament or Inside Olympics game on Friday. Allow each student to select a name or flag. Everyone will participate. Questions will be individualized to maximize success. A snack and possibly a sports video can be made available after the game as a reward.

Math, Science, and Social Studies

Proceed with the studies initiated previously. These studies can evolve into a new unit of study or end with the culminating event described in the Reading and Language Arts section of Week 5.

STAGE TWO THEME: PLANTS

Stage Two planning requires a focus on transitional skills required for effective cooperative efforts. Students will need to be monitored carefully as they apply social skills to dyad teams. The following overviews are divided into elementary-level and middle-/high-school-level plans. A list of possible reading materials for each level and sample worksheets and activities are provided for teacher use.

AFFECTIVE BULLETIN BOARD

The seedling nursery can be a starting point for developing an affective bulletin board. Each student can have a plant with leaves or petals that describe positive behaviors. A tree can be developed that illustrates the strengths of each member of the class and the positive interdependence created when each person contributes in an appropriate way.

READINGS

Elementary Level

Jack and the Beanstalk (Traditional)

The Sunflower Garden by J. M. Udry

What Makes Popcorn Pop? by David Woodside

Why Corn Is Golden by Vivien Blackmore

Stone Soup (Traditional)

Middle School/High School Level

The Plant Doctor by Mary C. Lewis

A Plant Person by J. R. Gardiner

Paul Bunyan's Cornstalk by H. Courlander

Have You Thanked a Green Plant Today? by Don Anderson

PLANTS: GERMINATION

Suggested Group Activities

1. Before assigning the project activities, a discussion of the science words and concepts involved, along with visual aids and/or a filmstrip, will prepare students to be more independent and creative in their work. Be sure to cover the meaning of germination, the scientific method of experimenting and recording the results, and how to use graphs. The questions on percentage can be done as a group if individual students are not ready to do that independently.

2. Language Arts.

   a. After a filmstrip and discussion of the science content material, a word wall can be developed of nouns, verbs, and modifiers. The sophistication of this activity can be adjusted to the needs of the group with individual assignments following the group discussion.

   b. Use the Fractured Fairytale provided. Ask for the parts of speech listed under the blanks before reading the story. Then read the story, filling in the blanks with the words given. You'll get a lot of laughs! This can be the start of student-made Fractured Fairytales.

3. Math. Set up a contest. Fill a jar with beans. Have each student estimate (a) the number of beans in the jar, (b) the weight of the beans, and (c) the length of the line the beans would make if they were lined up end to end. The winners for each category can decide on a special treat for the group.

4. Set up a plant adoption center. Prospective plant "parents" can select a seed of their choice. When the seed sprouts, the plant parent can receive an official Germination Certificate and a card with instructions on the care and feeding of the new little seedling. Each parent can then keep a chart of the plant's growth, use it for experiments, name it, use it for descriptive writing assignments, and so on.

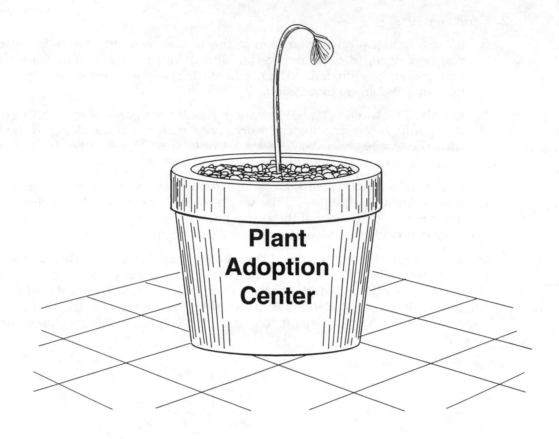

**Plant
Adoption
Center**

**Congratulations! You will soon be the
proud parent of a splendid seedling!**

SEEDLINGS

Source: *Back Off, Cool Down, Try Again*, Sylvia Rockwell, 1995, Reston, VA: The Council for Exceptional Children.

LANGUAGE ARTS: GERMINATION

Plants are living things, and they share some of the same needs for food, water, air, protection, and special environments as other living things. A discussion of this fact can lead students into a study of the specific needs, strengths, and weaknesses of their adopted plant.

Activity 1

Give the students several different types of birth announcements to examine. Have them design one to use when their seed germinates. Completed germination announcements can be displayed in the Plant Adoption Center along with Germination Certificates and Growth Charts.

Activity 2

After an introduction of science content material through discussion, film, or reading, a word wall can be developed of nouns, verbs, and modifiers. When introducing the concepts of nouns, the teacher might first ask for a list of *things* and later point out that these are all *nouns*. Instead of using the word *verb* initially, the teacher can ask the students to list words that tell what the "thing words" *do*. Modifiers can be referred to as *describing words*.

Sample Word Wall

Things (Nouns)	Actions (Verbs)	Describing Words (Adjectives & Adverbs)
plant	germinate	slowly
seed	sprout	tiny
plumule	grow	yellow

Extending Activities for the Word Wall

1. Alphabetize each word in each category.

2. Divide words into syllables.

3. Pantomime nouns and verbs.

4. Begin a class-made word bank or science dictionary.

5. Use the words in a student- or teacher-made word search or crossword puzzle. (See the examplc on page 114.)

6. Fractured Fairytales. (See the example on page 115.)

Germination Certificate

Seedling's Name _____

Parent's Name _____

Date _____

School _____

City _____   State _____

Attending Teacher's Signature

_____

Health Record Growth Chart

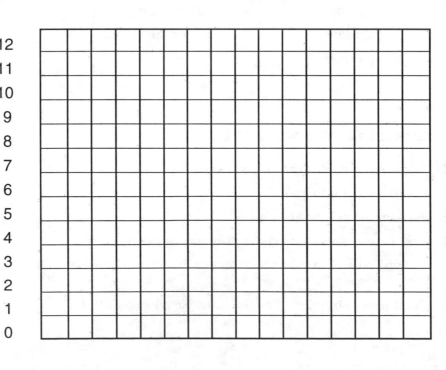

Units of Measure

12
11
10
9
8
7
6
5
4
3
2
1
0

Source: *Back Off, Cool Down, Try Again*, Sylvia Rockwell, 1995, Reston, VA: The Council for Exceptional Children.

FRACTURED FAIRYTALE

Jack and the Bean_____
(noun)

Once upon a time, there lived a poor old _____ and her _____. They had
(noun)   (noun)

very little to _____ and no _____ to _____ any. So Jack's _____
(verb)   (noun)   (verb)   (noun)

sent him off to _____.
(verb)

He was usually a _____ boy and _____ just as his mother asked.
(adjective)   (verb)

Unfortunately, on his way home, he met up with a _____ _____ who took his
(adjective)   (noun)

money and gave him some magic _____.
(plural noun)

When he got home, his mother was so angry she _____ them out the
(verb)

_____ and sent _____ to _____ without his _____.
(noun)   (noun)   (noun)   (noun)

Jack climbed the _____ _____ and discovered a _____
(adjective)   (noun)   (adjective)

_____.
(noun)

You finish the story in your own words.

Source: *Back Off, Cool Down, Try Again*, Sylvia Rockwell, 1995, Reston, VA: The Council for Exceptional Children.

MATH: GERMINATION

HORIZONTAL BAR GRAPH

If you were a plant, you might celebrate your germination day—the day you became a sprout!

Ask 12 people the month of their birth. Color one square next to the correct month for each person you ask.

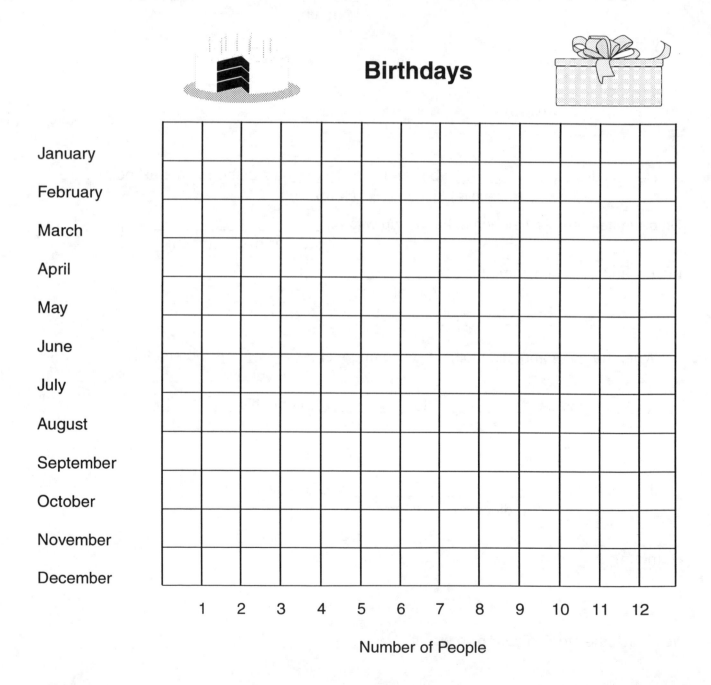

LINE GRAPH

Ask 15 people how many people are in their family. For each, put a dot where the line for the person meets the line for the number of people.

Number of People in Family

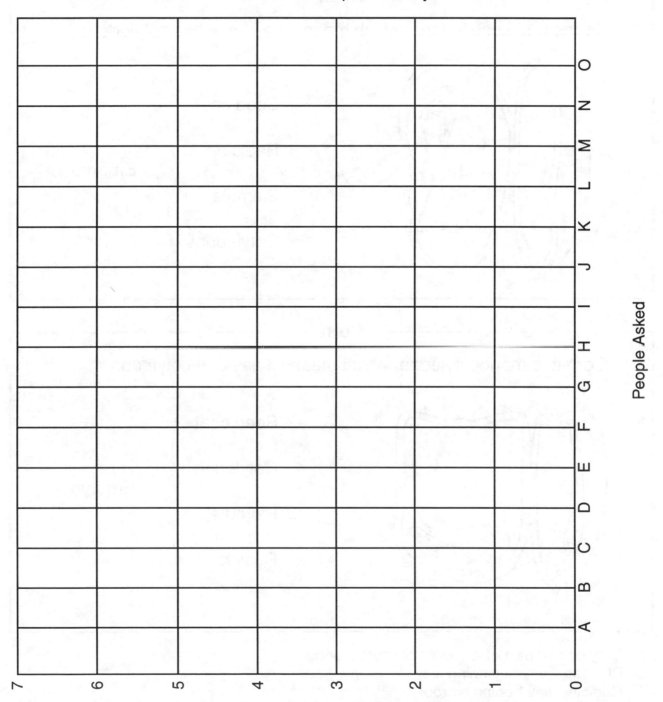

People Asked

Source: *Back Off, Cool Down, Try Again*, Sylvia Rockwell, 1995, Reston, VA: The Council for Exceptional Children.

GERMINATION

Seeds germinate or sprout when conditions are right. The hard seed coat protects the embryo plant until the seed is in a warm, moist environment.

Bean

Beans are dicotyledons, which means they have two cotyledons.

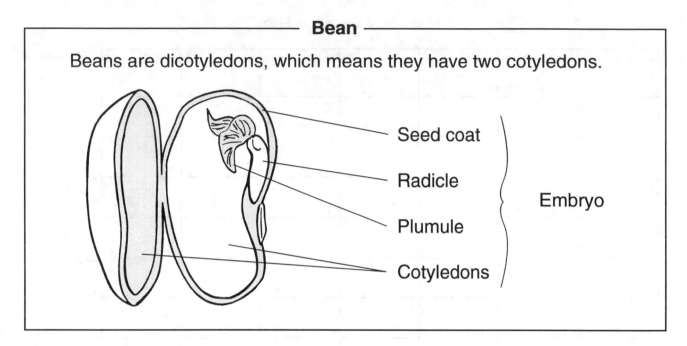

Corn

Corn is a monocotyledon, which means it has one cotyledon.

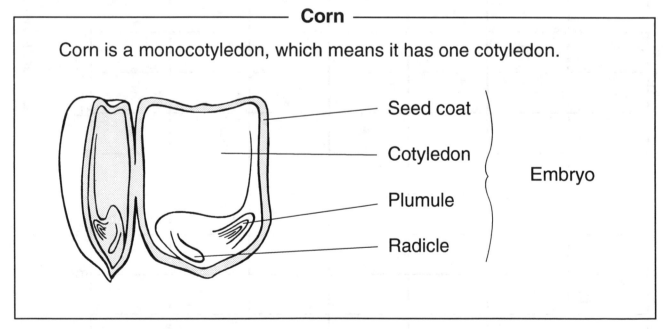

1. Cotyledon—part of a seed with stored food.
2. Plumule—tiny beginning leaf.
3. Radicle—tiny beginning root
4. Embryo—tiny sleeping plant.
5. Seed coat—hard shell around embryo.

Source: *Back Off, Cool Down, Try Again*, Sylvia Rockwell, 1995, Reston, VA: The Council for Exceptional Children.

GERMINATION ACTIVITIES

Select two or more of the following:

1. Make a detailed sketch of three or four different types of seeds that have been soaked and split. Label each of the parts.

2. Write down as many words of three or more letters as can be made with the letters in GERMINATION.

3. Do some research to find out how many different seeds man uses. Make a poster to illustrate the different uses.

4. Use different types of seeds to make a mosaic.

5. Make up a game that could be played with seeds. Teach it to the class.

Source: *Back Off, Cool Down, Try Again*, Sylvia Rockwell, 1995, Reston, VA: The Council for Exceptional Children.

PLANTS: TROPISMS

Suggested Group Activities

1. A group discussion of the different types of tropisms with the use of visual aids and/or a filmstrip, movie, and reading material should precede any individual work.

2. Math. Tropisms can be negative or positive. A discussion of this fact can lead into the meaning of positive and negative integers and/or deficits and assets in keeping a checkbook, bookkeeping, and business.

3. Language Arts.

   a. After the group fully understands the meaning of antonyms and synonyms, a word wall can be developed with student-made illustrations.

   b. See the Scrambled "Multinyms" worksheet included.

   c. Discuss how plants and animals are alike and how they differ. Have students draw or construct with wire, cloth, yarn, or other materials imaginary plants that are able to do everything animals do.

   d. Using the imaginary plant creatures, make up a filmstrip, skit, or puppet show about the eggplant that ate Chicago.

TROPISM ACTIVITIES

1. Make up an experiment using what you know about tropisms to prove that plants move.

2. With a partner, test your word power by describing a plant your partner can't see and asking him to draw it based on your description. Then reverse the roles.

3. Tropisms can be positive or negative. Plants move toward or away from certain things. Words are alike or opposite in meanings. Words that are alike are called *synonyms*. Words that are opposite in meaning are called *antonyms*. Find antonyms and synonyms for the following words:

shiny	tall	bright
big	thin	floppy
rough	leafy	strong

Then describe a living thing and let a friend guess the thing you described.

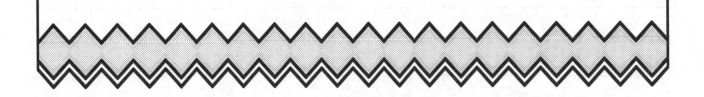

Source: *Back Off, Cool Down, Try Again,* Sylvia Rockwell, 1995, Reston, VA: The Council for Exceptional Children.

SCRAMBLED MULTINYMS

Unscramble all the words below. Then put them in the appropriate columns.

ropo	itny
ruep	dsa
nem	elmafe
aterg	futbielua
lwufa	papyh
kdra	ldwacoyr
eghu	eoauuosgrc
latl	guyl
ionlmuus	adb
lwyhtae	torhs

	Synonyms	Antonyms
small		
lofty		
male		
joyful		
bright		
good		
evil		
brave		
rich		
pretty		

Source: *Back Off, Cool Down, Try Again*, Sylvia Rockwell, 1995, Reston, VA: The Council for Exceptional Children.

PLANTS: STRUCTURE

Suggested Group Activities

1. Collect berries to make dye to use in dying cloth for book covers.

2. Compare the parts of the human body to the parts of plants. This comparison can be very simple (e.g., the trunk of a tree is like the torso of the body) or fairly sophisticated (e.g., xylem and phloem are like veins and arteries). An introduction to this unit can begin with a filmstrip on the parts of plants. Using the comparison activity as a follow-up would reinforce the new information presented. An art activity— drawing or constructing a plant creature—could follow as an introduction to a creative writing assignment about plants.

3. Dissect a flower to identify the parts.

4. Collect plants to represent the diagrams on the next page.

5. Talk about root words. The *di* in dicotyledon means two. The *mono* in monocotyledon means one. The students can think of other words they know with prefixes that represent numbers. This discussion could also be part of a math lesson on shapes. One of the project activities deals with this.

PLANT STRUCTURE

Suggested Activities

1. Plants have a circulatory system that has some similarities to our own. Find out more about it. Make a diagram or two to illustrate what you learn.

2. What is *photosynthesis*? Where does it take place? What makes it happen? Draw pictures and write a paragraph or two about it.

3. Transpiration is something like a plant's respiratory system. Find out what that means. Do an experiment to prove it.

4. Research the common peanut plant. Find out how many uses man has found for each part of the plant. Share what you learn with a display, puppet show, and/or pictures.

5. You can tell many things about a tree's life by reading the rings in a cross section or "cookie." Find out how to do this and demonstrate your knowledge to the group.

Select two or more of these activities or create some of your own after checking with your teacher.

Source: *Back Off, Cool Down, Try Again*, Sylvia Rockwell, 1995, Reston, VA: The Council for Exceptional Children.

PLANTS: IDENTIFICATION

Suggested Group Activities

1. Accompany the group on a guided nature ramble.

2. Conduct a plant identification interview. (See the instruction sheet on the next page.)

3. Set up a "Wanted Dead or Alive" poster in the classroom. Post the names of poisonous plants found in the area on the poster. Students can then research the plants, find out how to identify them, the effects of the poison, and how to treat a person who has contacted or consumed the plant.

4. Play a "Guess Who?" game to encourage the development of descriptive language. Have each person select a plant to describe. After the student describes it orally, the group can ask questions or make a guess. The person who guesses correctly wins the opportunity to describe his or her plant. After oral descriptions become more fluent, let partners draw what they think the other person is describing and evaluate accuracy of speaking as well as listening skills. The final step would be written descriptions. The written descriptions can then be used in a group-developed plant book complete with pictures and diagrams.

PLANT IDENTIFICATION ACTIVITIES

1. Scientists divide the world of living things into two broad categories, plants and animals. Find out how the plant kingdom is subdivided. Make a chart to illustrate what you learn.

2. Make crayon rubbings of several different types of leaves found in your area. Set up a display and challenge others in the group to identify them. Let people write their guesses on a sheet of paper posted under each rubbing. At the end of the week, reveal the correct answers.

3. Make up cards with plant names on them. Give each person in the room a card. One person at a time must act out the plant name without using words. The group tries to guess the plant name.

4. Find out more about poisonous plants. Some plants you would not suspect have poisonous parts. Would you believe that parts of a peach tree can kill if eaten? Share what you learn with the group.

5. Make a map of your area. Identify the types of plants commonly found.

Select two or more of these activities or create some of your own.

Source: *Back Off, Cool Down, Try Again*, Sylvia Rockwell, 1995, Reston, VA: The Council for Exceptional Children.

PLANT INTERVIEW

Have three to five students go to the front of the room. Before starting, ask them to think of a plant they would like to be and assume a physical posture representative of that plant. Then ask the following questions or ones you have prepared. Allow each person to respond to each question before going to the next. Do not start with the same person every time.

Interview questions should be a mixture of fantasy and fact-related types. This activity stimulates a lot of creative conversation.

Sample Interview

1. Each of you is a plant. Assume the position that best represents you.

2. How would you identify you? What do you look like?

3. What is your favorite environment? Where do you live?

4. Who are your friends?

5. Who are your enemies?

6. If you were to be used for some famous discovery, what would it be?

Source: *Back Off, Cool Down, Try Again*, Sylvia Rockwell, 1995, Reston, VA: The Council for Exceptional Children.

PLANTS

```
C  A  B  A  N  T  H  E  R  S  C  D  E  M  E  O  L  H  P
L  F  P  H  O  T  O  S  Y  N  T  H  E  S  I  S  G  H  I
A  J  K  L  I  M  N  O  P  Q  R  E  L  C  I  D  A  R  S
S  S  T  U  T  F  A  R  G  V  W  X  Y  Z  A  C  B  I  T
S  D  F  E  C  S  G  I  H  V  A  C  U  O  L  E  S  T  I
I  J  L  K  A  T  N  M  P  O  P  Q  R  L  S  O  A  R  L
F  T  U  V  Y  O  W  S  L  Y  X  Z  Y  A  M  O  B  O  C
I  D  N  N  R  M  L  E  A  F  E  H  F  S  C  G  I  P  H
C  E  O  O  A  A  J  E  N  K  P  L  O  D  M  O  P  I  N
A  L  I  D  L  T  Q  D  T  O  O  R  E  R  M  E  T  S  N
T  U  T  E  L  A  S  T  R  Y  P  E  T  A  L  S  V  M  U
I  M  A  L  I  T  U  O  V  R  S  W  X  W  Y  Z  E  S  C
O  U  R  Y  P  A  L  C  B  B  C  O  F  D  E  L  I  G  L
N  L  I  T  A  H  J  I  H  M  I  L  K  M  Y  L  N  N  E
O  P  P  O  C  P  Q  D  R  E  T  F  S  X  U  W  V  X  U
Y  A  S  C  Z  C  B  N  O  I  T  S  E  G  I  D  D  E  S
S  E  E  D  L  I  N  G  F  H  G  I  T  O  C  O  N  O  M
J  L  R  G  E  R  M  I  N  A  T  I  O  N  K  M  O  P  S
```

ANTHER	LEAF	RESPIRATION
CAPILLARY ACTION	MONOCOT	ROOT
CHLOROPHYLL	NUCLEUS	SEED
CLASSIFICATION	OSMOSIS	SEED COAT
COTYLEDON	PETALS	SEEDLING
DICOT	PHLOEM	STEM
DIGESTION	PISTIL	STOMATA
EMBRYO	PHOTOSYNTHESIS	TROPISM
FLOWER	PLANT	VACUOLE
GERMINATION	PLUMULE	VEIN
GRAFT	RADICLE	XYLEM

Source: *Back Off, Cool Down, Try Again,* Sylvia Rockwell, 1995, Reston, VA: The Council for Exceptional Children.

NUTRITION

Suggested Group Activities

1. Plan cook-out menus to include daily requirements of the four basic food groups.

2. Collect and study content information on canned and other packaged food. Then make a collage of them.

3. Write letters to food companies about processing, labeling, and nutrient requirements.

4. Have a brainstorming session to develop an original, healthy super snack.

5. Test foods for vitamin C, starch, and oil.

6. Discuss diseases that result from vitamin and mineral deficiencies. Prepare a chuckwagon skit to teach others about the risks of an improper diet.

NUTRITION ACTIVITIES

1. Find out what the suggested daily caloric intake is for your age group. Keep track of your diet for a week and check it for calories as well as nutrition.

2. Make a chart showing good sources of the following vitamins and health problems that result from deficiencies: A, D, B_1 (thiamin), B_2 (riboflavin), B_6 (niacin), and C (ascorbic acid).

3. Test the effects of heat on vitamin C. Heat portions of the juice from an orange. Check for vitamin C at different temperatures.

4. Make a report to the group on different food fads or diet fads that are potentially harmful.

5. With the help of others in the group, make a recipe book of healthy as well as delicious meals and snacks. (Any recipe that is new to the group should be tested before including it in the cookbook.)

6. Make a chart grouping foods we eat according to the part of the plant that is edible. For instance, we eat the stem of celery, the roots of carrots, and the leaves of cabbage.

Select two of the suggested activities or make up two of your own after checking with your teacher.

Source: *Back Off, Cool Down, Try Again,* Sylvia Rockwell, 1995, Reston, VA: The Council for Exceptional Children.

STAGE THREE THEME: ECONOMICS

By the time a group has reached Stage Three functioning, cooperative ventures should be routine. This unit allows students to work together in a variety of ways. They move well beyond mere memorization of facts with authentic opportunities to evaluate decisions based on facts and personal preferences. As much as I would like to preach at times, I have found that the best way to get a point across is to lead students to their own level of understanding. Before I share a plan that has worked numerous times with students in grades 4 through 12, a few experiences with students and parents are in order.

In one middle school class, the boys started this unit of study with great enthusiasm. They were all going to be marvelously wealthy without going to school or working more than 30 hours per week. As they called businesses found in the classified section of the newspaper and established entry-level requirements and wages, their excitement continued to mount. Five dollars an hour sounded like plenty of money to them. One particular student, named Andy, began to tell me daily of his plan to wine and dine his girlfriend. According to Andy, a stretch limousine would take them to fancy restaurants every evening. They would go to movies and concerts dressed in the latest fashions. Lavish parties with friends would be routine. I smiled and truly enjoyed his fantasy. I asked him to keep me posted on this dream life as he continued through the project. On the last day, just before the class met to discuss their results, Andy pulled me aside and asked, "Do you remember the stretch limousines, fancy dinners at restaurants, movies, concerts, and fancy clothes?" I replied that I did. He continued with, "Well, I've had a change of plans. With this job, I'll be riding my girl on the handlebars of my bike. We'll rent a movie and watch it on the couch while we eat microwave popcorn." We both had a good laugh. His mother reported to me later that the whole family got involved with this project. Many dinner-time conversations were centered around jobs, consumer issues, and the benefits of completing school. When academic work leads naturally into the family and community, motivating students to learn, collaborate with others, and work creatively toward a resolution is effortless.

This unit is most effective if combined with field trips to a bank, a grocery store, and a department store. Guest speakers on related topics enhance learning as well. A description of each week's focus follows.

STAGE THREE THEME: ECONOMICS

Day 1

The manner in which this unit is presented to students is important. The activities provided are intrinsically motivating. Well-meaning adults can, however, dampen enthusiasm by trying to insert the constraints of reality prematurely. Let the students dream! They will have wild and totally unrealistic ideas about what they can do. The activities required in the project packet will surprise them. It is wise to let experience be the teacher. They will meet the demands of the real world with renewed determination and creative problem-solving strategies if their dreams are honored. Do not tell them they cannot reach a particular goal. Ask instead how they will get there.

Begin by presenting each student with a project coversheet (provided on page 133). Explain that the students will be responsible for developing a completed monthly budget based on entry-level wages at a job of their choice and the current market rates for utilities, housing, food, entertainment, and so forth. Two to four students may work together to pool resources for certain expenses. If they decide to share a car, house, or apartment, they will need to describe the nature of the agreement and the schedules and guidelines all will follow. Who will cook? Who will clean? Who will pay the bills? How will food be purchased? Who will take care of repairs? What will happen if someone does not live up to the agreement? It is a good idea to have a culminating activity planned.

Because play money and checks are used, I like to offer a special classroom store for the purchase of items students have really wanted during the year. Students may spend any money that is left from one month's wages after taxes, living expenses, and 5% savings have been subtracted. They must prove that they have sufficient funds to cover the purchase, and they must write the check accurately. A class meeting to discuss favorite activities, important insights, and future plans is an essential culminating component as well.

Week 1

Students will use the classified section of the newspaper to find employment, transportation, and housing. Categorizing and generating possible keywords for referencing information will be a challenge for some students. Common abbreviations used in classified advertisements will also be of interest. As students select jobs and housing, they will need to use a map and consider transportation to and from work. Project entries for Week 1 could include a newspaper clipping describing a desired job; documentation of the telephone call made to inquire about entry-level wages, requirements, and responsibilities; a newspaper clipping describing a desired rental property; documentation of a telephone call made to inquire about deposits; a list of abbreviations and keywords used; a map of the city with the route to and from work highlighted; and the appropriate sections of the monthly budget sheet completed.

Week 2

During Week 2, students will continue to explore local opportunities for consumer education. Their personal interests can be sources for research. The monthly budget sheet has sections for entertainment, insurance, and car repair and maintenance. Students will need to identify the places they plan to frequent, prices for services desired, and transportation routes and methods. Finding percentages will be important in computing sales tax and income tax. Knowing the difference between gross pay and net pay will be required in project planning. Week 2 documentation can include highlighted maps; addresses and phone numbers of insurance companies, repair and maintenance shops, and entertainment spots; computation of net and gross pay; computation of sales tax; and a teacher-made telephone book scavenger hunt.

Week 3

The literature suggested for Week 3 would be a nonfiction selection by Kathlyn Gay titled *Be a Smart Shopper*. A trip to a grocery store and a department store to do comparison shopping for foods and clothing would be helpful this week. Grocery advertisements in the newspaper can be used to price grocery list items, and clothing catalogs can be used to project clothing needs. Actually going to the stores with the students gives the teacher an opportunity to demonstrate more realistically the variables that must be considered in deciding on a particular purchase. For example, while the large economy size might be cheaper per ounce, if only one person will be consuming the specific food item, will it spoil before it can be used? With clothing, students need to be shown which fabrics are easy to care for and are most durable. Price and style are only two of many factors that should be considered. Project entries for Week 3 could include a weekly menu and grocery list; a monthly budget for food; a projected yearly and monthly allotment for clothing; criteria for making purchases based on consumer education information and personal preferences; sample newspaper and magazine advertisements depicting different tactics used to attempt to convince people to purchase certain items; examples of consumer computation problems; and information on possible retail sales occupations.

Week 4

The Shepherd's Treasure by Mark Morano can be used to explore prediction and making inferences with fiction. The message of this selection and that of the suggested story for Week 4 point to an examination of values beyond consumerism. While students learn to fill out forms, keep banking registers, visit a bank, and continue to deal with budgeting issues, discussions can arise concerning the values of friendship, family, health, and other less tangible necessities of life. Project entries for Week 4 can include a personal essay on values money cannot buy; examples of forms, registers, and applications accurately completed; and a description of the field trip to the bank.

Week 5

The Gift by Helen Coutant is another fiction selection that leads students to examine the values of family, friendship, health, and everyday pleasures. A comparison of this and *The Shepherd's Treasure* can be done on a Venn diagram. Project packets should be completed and displayed. Time to share and celebrate is important. Students will have gained many new insights and skills through this project that will remain with them beyond the present school term.

Name _____ Due Date _____

ECONOMICS PROJECT

The following list of assignments and activities has been developed to help you learn to plan a monthly budget, gain valuable consumer information, and explore entry-level job opportunities available to high school graduates. While working on this project, pretend that you are 18 years old and have just graduated from high school. All items listed and worksheets provided must be completed for full credit. Other assignments may be included in your portfolio at the request of the teacher. You are encouraged to add your own items of interest as well. Have fun as you fast-forward yourself into the future!

Project Requirements

1. Select a job from the classified section of the newspaper. Call the business. Explain that you are working on a class project. Ask about entry-level requirements, pay, and benefits. Record this information in a journal.

2. Select a house or apartment from the classified section of the newspaper. Make sure that your housing is near your work by using a city map. Call the rental office. Ask about deposits and monthly payments. Record this information in your journal.

3. Call utility and telephone companies. Ask about deposits and monthly fees.

4. Develop a full set of meal plans for 7 days. Make a grocery list. Price items. Compare generic and store-brand prices to brand-name prices. Record these in your journal.

5. Write down a list of clothes that you will need for recreation and work for 1 year. Price these items. Compare discount and brand-name prices. Divide the yearly cost by 12 to get a monthly clothing allowance. Record this in your journal.

6. Compute net pay and gross pay for one month.

7. Compute 5% of your net pay to put in a savings account.

8. Decide on the number and types of activities you will participate in for fun. Locate these places on a map. Compute the cost of transportation and participation. Record these items in your journal.

9. Add all expenses for a month, including money placed in savings.

10. Subtract the amount of expenses from your net pay. If the expense amount is greater than the net pay amount, look at the expenses again. Find some way to save money so that all bills can be paid.

11. Complete the sample bank register.

12. Write checks to all businesses listed on your expense worksheet.

13. Make written agreements about the house or car rules and schedules if you plan to share one of those items with a classmate.

Source: *Back Off, Cool Down, Try Again*, Sylvia Rockwell, 1995, Reston, VA: The Council for Exceptional Children.

EXPENSE WORKSHEET

Name _____   Job _____

Place of Employment   _____

Gross Annual Wages   _____   Net Pay _____

Gross Monthly Wages   _____   Net Pay _____

Monthly Rent   _____

Water   _____

Electricity   _____

Gas   _____

Garbage   _____

Car Payment   _____

Car Insurance   _____

Renter's Insurance   _____

Car Repairs and Maintenance   _____

Gas for the Car   _____

Food per Month (Multiply 1 week by 4.)   _____

Telephone   _____

Entertainment   _____

Health Insurance   _____

Clothing   _____

Savings (5%)   _____

TOTAL EXPENSES   _____

Subtract your total expenses from your monthly net pay.

What is your balance before being paid the next month? _____

Source: *Back Off, Cool Down, Try Again*, Sylvia Rockwell, 1995, Reston, VA: The Council for Exceptional Children.

WEEKLY MENU

Remember to include all four food groups.

	Breakfast	Lunch	Dinner	Snacks
Monday				
Tuesday				
Wednesday				
Thursday				
Friday				
Saturday				
Sunday				

Source: *Back Off, Cool Down, Try Again*, Sylvia Rockwell, 1995, Reston, VA: The Council for Exceptional Children.

GROCERY LIST

Item*		Brand Name Price	Generic Price	Item*		Brand Name Price	Generic Price
				TOTAL			
				Multiply by 4 to get the monthly cost.			

*soap, deodorant, etc. Also seasonings and condiments.

Source: *Back Off, Cool Down, Try Again*, Sylvia Rockwell, 1995, Reston, VA: The Council for Exceptional Children.

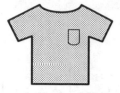

CLOTHING WORKSHEET

	Name Brand	Budget Priced
Underwear (6 pair)	_____	_____
Socks (6 pair)	_____	_____
T-shirts (6)	_____	_____
Dress shoes	_____	_____
Tennis shoes	_____	_____
Heavy coat	_____	_____
Light jacket	_____	_____
Swimsuit	_____	_____
Jeans (5 pairs)	_____	_____
Workclothes	_____	_____
_____	_____	_____
_____	_____	_____
_____	_____	_____
_____	_____	_____
_____	_____	_____
_____	_____	_____
TOTALS	_____	_____
Divide by 12 for monthly cost	_____	_____

Source: *Back Off, Cool Down, Try Again*, Sylvia Rockwell, 1995, Reston, VA: The Council for Exceptional Children.

BANK REGISTER

Deposit Ticket

Name _____

Date _____

Signature _____

Cash	
Checks	
Total	

Number	Date	Description of Transaction	Payment Debit (−)	Fee (−)	Deposit Credit (+)	Balance
		5% of total monthly income for savings				

Source: *Back Off, Cool Down, Try Again*, Sylvia Rockwell, 1995, Reston, VA: The Council for Exceptional Children.

Name

Street

City, State, Zip

Check No.

_____ 19 _____

Pay to the order of _____ $ [   ]

_____ Dollars

COPPERSMITH FIRST NATIONAL
FIRST ST. &   TORTULA,
LOBO AVE.   CALIFORNIA

MEMO_____

1:00000000:1   123" L56"7811:   0000

Name

Street

City, State, Zip

Check No.

_____ 19 _____

Pay to the order of _____ $ [   ]

_____ Dollars

COPPERSMITH FIRST NATIONAL
FIRST ST. &   TORTULA,
LOBO AVE.   CALIFORNIA

MEMO_____

1:00000000:1   123" L56"7811:   0000

Name

Street

City, State, Zip

Check No.

_____ 19 _____

Pay to the order of _____ $ [   ]

_____ Dollars

COPPERSMITH FIRST NATIONAL
FIRST ST. &   TORTULA,
LOBO AVE.   CALIFORNIA

MEMO_____

1:00000000:1   123" L56"7811:   0000